Let Go of your But!

Heartistic Motivation
Presents

HM

Creating Possibilities From Within

Let Go of Your But!

For women who are ready to create new possibilities from within

The Let Go of Your But! Motivational Series

is written by

Kimberly E. Banks

Let Go of your But!

ISBN - 978-0-578-04999-1

Management@HeartisticMotivation.com

1-866-377-7265 or (678)999-6337

Heartistic Motivation

www.HeartisticMotivation.com

Let Go Of Your But!™

www.LetGoOfYourBut.com

Inside This Book

Let Go of your But!

There is nothing to one feared within the Creator's Presence

Reader's affirmations of Divine support and will:

I AM all there is.
I HAVE unlimited potential.
I AM greater than fears or challenges.
I AM more than my illness and discomfort.
I HAVE the power to create my life exactly as I envision.
I AM worthy of love, joy, friendship and healthy relationships.
I CHOOSE to move forward, seeking and sharing positive energy.
I TRUST all my choices and decision because I am mindful and aligned.
I AM always capable of overcoming all that impede the flow of abundance.
I AVAIL myself to learning, growing, and being accountable for all that
occurs in my life.
I AM truth
I AM free.
I AM love.
I AM wise.
I AM peace.
I AM joyful.
I AM the great I AM.
I AM rooted in mindfulness.
I WELCOME and embrace change.
I SUCCEED in whatever I chose to do
I AM and have everything I need, right now.
I AM always the relationship I am having with others
TODAY, I patiently nurture seeds that will become a tree in my tomorrow.

**NOTE FOR READER: Be aware that the content in this book gets
progressively more challenging as the chapters unfold. I have designed
this project in this fashion to raise the bar of women who are ready to
create new possibilities in their lives. This is my effort to empower you to
grow new roots for the beginning of your journey as your true self.**

Acknowledgements

Women of Power!

*L*et Go of your But was written in memory of a beloved angel, Kimberly Harpe, who is now in heaven and hopefully smiling down on me, and the world she transcended. I felt compelled to start a project like this because it was through you that I was able to witness a living example of how one should find joy in all things and the people they encounter throughout the time between their first and last breaths. Now that you have your wings, I too can smile wide knowing that you are somewhere in the Universe spreading kindness, sharing love, singing your heart out and living the life you aspired to live when you were here. I only wish you were here to see the changes that have manifest in my own life subsequent to your departure. I miss you!

Nicole Thomas, I dedicate a large part of this effort to you because it was your presence that enabled me to finish this book so that my words may be shared with the Universe. You were the spark I needed to re-ignite my flame when I was surrounded by grief. Fortunately, I am forever enthused by the task of carrying out my purpose, so that I might be the model of the change I wish to see in this world. This is my contribution. You helped me remember the abundance of love that dwells at the center of my heart in spite of all that I have endured. Now, I am compelled to use all that I have experienced to be an inspiration to others through the gifts and talents with which I have been born. I hope that someday you are inspired to tell your own story, so that others may be able to comprehend exactly why my light shines brighter today. You have definitely taught me to look beyond the circumstances and to stay focused on the desired outcome. I couldn't ask for more. Thanks so much for your friendship and support.

Barbara Dyce and Angela Burris…thanks for lifting me up in the light of your belief in the actualization of my intended self. Though you are not always in my presence, your support has been greatly appreciated.

Most importantly…my mother, Rena DeJarentte. I couldn't have done this without you! Thanks for having me and instilling within me the will to strive and persevere. Who knew I would be here today.

And to all the women who have encouraged me to go after my dreams. Thanks for believing in me. Thanks for shedding light on my purpose and holding me accountable to "walk the walk" even when I couldn't see the things you saw things in me. Thanks for pushing me to "Let Go of MY But!"

"The journey of 1,000 miles begins right beneath your feet."
– Lao Tzu

Let Go of your But!

The Journey Begins Here

*A*t last, I have found you. It is my belief that our connection is not an outlandish coincidence, randomly occurring within the scheme of your earthly existence. The Universe is always at work under the dynamic command of "ask and you shall receive" or in a scholastic analogy, "when the student is ready, the teacher will come." Considering the significance of the fact that this book has made it into your possession, let us both assume and/or conclude that you are at a point in your life where you have opened your heart wide enough to recognize and welcome the change that is necessary for the evolution that is YOUR life.

Congratulations! I commend you for ensuing the notion to let go of your "but" so that you may endeavor to reach for the things that you have been too afraid to pursue on account of potential failure. Maybe, as a woman, letting go of your but has nothing to do with overcoming fear. Maybe you are tired of being sick and tired of having lack in your life and are ready to pursue avenues that will bring financial increase. Possibly, you're simply exhausted from watching life pass you by. Or, quite possibly you're bored with your current circumstances and need to find a way to feel alive again. Let's say you are a woman of ambition, submerged in an abyss of prejudiced men who feel as though your presence is much better suited for catering to their needs as they climb the golden rungs of the corporate ladder – a ladder that if left up to them would be completely off limits to you. Or maybe you have this great idea nestled inside your heart and seeing as you have all these other shoes to fill – role of mother, daughter, head of the household, provider, employee, etc. – you can't quite find the motivation you need to see your dreams through to fruition.

WHEW! What a mouthful…but I suppose you get my point.

Whatever the case may be, we all have aspirations – short term to long term, temporary to life-long intentions. Trust me when I say, they do not reside in the core of your heart without reason. Sometimes, we as women find ourselves at a point of reflection only to discover that we are somewhere other than where we desire to be or someone other than whom we wish to be. Sound familiar to you? Well…again, you can best believe that it is no twist of fate that you and I have crossed paths today. My sister, you are here sharing this moment with me as a result of your reaching a crossroad in your life. Striving to break the monotony of doing the same mundane tasks day after day after day after day…and halfway expecting different results has become exhausting to you. Aren't you ready for the cycle of insanity to cease? Are you ready for that monumental change of pace that will send you sailing full speed ahead toward prosperity and fulfillment?

Perfect! This is the perfect inspirational tool for you.

Once more, I'd like to commend you for taking that first step towards change and transformation. Creating the life you aspire to live takes work, however, realizing that change is necessary, is a process most people are not willing to undergo. As you will learn in later pages, in order to maintain your momentum towards your desired intentions, turning your thoughts into actions must become a key part of your everyday life. I really hope you will do more than just read the text on the following pages, but rather use this book as a tool to help you move through stagnation and into your desired place and purpose in life. Though not always easy, try your best not to be fooled by what can easily invoke depression, discontent, disappointment and discouragement! "Change how you look at things and the things you look at will change" quotes Dr. Wayne Dyer. We sometimes get caught in waiting for things to change; without

14

taking the time to change our perception of how things show up in our lives consequent to how we view ourselves. Everything we aspire to experience starts from within, not from the outside. So…this means that when we can shift our focus of attention, increase the amount of elbow grease used to polish our innermost self (which includes your emotions, thoughts, ideas, perceptions and beliefs) until gratitude and appreciation radiates from our hearts, all of our dreams can begin to unfold. The purpose of this book is to inspire you to live your life from the inside-out, not the outside-in; to empower you to believe that you have been designed to create your destiny…NO ONE ELSE…but…YOU!

Again, recognizing that you are stuck in a state of "changelessness" is a great accomplishment in itself. In the infamous inspirational movie The Secret, Dr. Joe Vitale says. "…A lot of people feel stuck, confined, or imprisoned by their current circumstances…whatever your circumstances right now, that is only your current reality." Our current realities begin to change the moment we invest the time to start changing our perceptions, expectations, actions, speech and focus. In order to change your circumstances, you must change your thinking. He goes on to say, "Most people look at their current state of affairs and say 'this is who I am.' That's not who you are, it's who you were. Your current state of affairs are the residuals of your past thoughts and actions."

There are plenty of people in this world who remain bound by misery without a chance for escape simply because they refuse to take inventory as to why and how their lives became sedentary in the first place. I mean this without judgment to those who find comfort in riding the hamster wheel leading nowhere; however, this obviously is no longer the case for you.

Still, in order to reach success (understanding of course that success is relative to each individual) it is imperative that we as women recognize that there are different degrees of stagnation when it comes to striving for a better life and lifestyle. If you have any ounce of ambition inside you, it is quite likely that there has been a time or two where you felt as though you were standing knee deep in quicksand, without a supporting hand to which you could cling. Even worst, the courage you need to take advantage of the resources and possibilities that surround seem unapparent or non-existent. Trapped in such a compromising position, it is no wonder you feel like a person bound in a straight jacket without any clues as to how to break free from feeling as though you are being robbed of your opportunity for escape.

Truthfully, deciphering where you fit in the aforementioned scenarios is moot; since you are on the path to overcoming excuses, challenges and obstacles, circumstances are of no relevance at this stage of the game. What matters most at this very moment...right here, right now...is that you have arrived to the place where change begins! The good news is that the time for adjustment has reared its beautiful little head. It has presented itself as inspiration for you to push yourself over the mountain of fear you've created in your mind. There she stands, waiting on higher ground, excited and encouraged, offering you an outstretched hand to pull you out of darkness.

Okay...I have something very profound to share - both "good" and "bad." Well, the bad news is that after reading this book, you will no longer be able to use the same silly excuses you have been using up until this point: "But...I didn't know how to do this...But, I don't know where to start...But, I don't have the means, the time, the money..."

The BUTS stop here.

Today, you will make the choice to do away with such nonsense. You will realize that excuses are merely conditions you have created in your mind, recorded and played over and over again so that you can justify your failure to act. More importantly, you will discover that much of this conditioning has been placed upon you by external forces – society, parents, teachers, politicians, etc. – whose successes have also been altered as a result of following belief systems that were passed down to them.

Get my point?

Today is a new day! On this day you will begin to pursue your own individuality, your own beliefs and your own concepts that are conducive to your wellbeing. You are now going to follow your own spirit in order to fulfill everything you are meant to become through the use of your own ideas, passions, talents and desires.

The good news is that the insight imparted onto the pages of this book is designed to motivate you to "let go of your but" and reach for your life – the life that rightfully belongs to you. Understand that realizing a dream is not something that happens overnight. However, you may find that self-actualization is right around the corner; the personification of your envisioned self may happen much sooner that you think. My suggestion is that you learn to focus your attention on grand possibility, as you are about to take your first step into a journey towards manifesting the desires of our heart.

Time is no longer an issue. Age is no longer an issue. The void of resources is no longer an issue. Family, school, bosses, children, jobs, etc...none of these people, places or things (or lack thereof) are viable obstacles or impediments that can keep you from success any longer.

Before we continue on this exciting path, please allow me to disclose a few intimate thoughts with you; thoughts that I am hoping will aid in getting you geared up for all that you are about to learn throughout this short, yet, significant time that we will share together.

A few years ago, I was speaking with a dear friend of mine – a loyal and kindhearted friend who believes in being honest to the umpteenth degree – when I was made aware of my propensity to use the conjunction "but" in the middle of my sentences during our exchanges. I can assume that if I used "but" during our conversations, I most likely used it in all of my conversations. Instinctively, I grew defensive, especially as thoughts of my elementary school days began to flash before my eyes. I remember so well how my fourth grade teacher, Ms. Miller, often scolded my classmates and me for using "but" or "I can't" whenever we were chosen to answer a problem or resolve a classroom matter. To say the least, I found myself standing in front of my friend horrified by the perception I must have presented on a regular basis.

In my mind, I was a positive and insightful person. Some would even add that I was wise and enlightened beyond my years. True, I had my challenges at the times, several in fact, "but", (there it goes again) I'd also accrued some monumental accomplishments in recent years; at least enough to eradicate any perceptions of being an underachiever. Apparently! I was wrong. Suddenly, the thought of me using "but" in every sentence seemed so appalling; atrocious even. I'd done so much in my life (already), so how was it possible that I'd grown accustomed to spewing such limiting dialogue. I'd traveled across country, produced television shows, wrote books and plenty of articles, started my own online publication, and used my artistic skills to create greeting cards and athletic apparel. I'd even hosted a couple of radio programs. How was it possible that such a word had infiltrated my widely expanded vocabulary repertoire?

Fathoming the possibility that I had become my very own obstacle was horrifying. In fact, it was completely unacceptable.

From that moment forward, I began listening to myself whenever I spoke and was quite shocked to discover that he'd been right. "Buts" decorated my conversations like little chocolate sprinkles on rounded mounds of ice cream. I once heard a supervisor cite to a group of subordinates, "...a 'but' negates everything that comes before it..." I took this to mean that anything I claimed I wanted to achieve vanished the moment word "but" came out of my mouth. The irony to this is that normally, when we hear the word "but" we tend to think of a big hunk of meat sitting on our backsides, inadvertently following us everywhere we go. Only my "buts" were not synonymous with the word behind. They actually served to be barriers standing before me. It was in that moment that I realized that in the proverbial mountain of buts, that no one other than myself had constructed, was a huge obstruction in the road leading towards my future.

In comparison to the self I envisioned throughout the better part of my adult life, I'd actually traveled very little distance on my path to success. I knew I was meant for greatness, but I didn't understand why, if I was putting such great effort into creating marvelous projects, I was not getting any closer to fulfilling my truest intentions. Reflecting further into the life I'd lived thus far, I soon was able to digest the reasoning behind my stagnation. That's when it finally dawned on me: I could have been much further in my dreams had I not been tiptoeing across pathways and shortcuts cluttered with "buts".

As much as it pained me to hear my friend's words and to accept such a reality, my life has since changed. To be honest, I wish I'd had this information much sooner. To this day, I still argue that I'd be so much further along in my stream of accomplishments if this had been the case. Yet, as the saying I mentioned earlier goes: "When the student is ready the master appears."

My story demonstrates how it wasn't until I was ready that I was able to become aware of the mistakes I'd been making.

I will reiterate the implication behind my last statement: As long as YOU continue to walk around with blinders covering your eyes, an obscured reality is all you will perceive. TRUTH and AWARENESS are the keys to achieving success. Thus, I encourage you to take a moment and ask yourself the following questions:

- Who am I?

  - Not who am I – now? But…WHO am I – really?

- What is the perception I hold of myself?

(Understand that the perception others may have of you may serve as a reference point. Try your best to dig deeper than the surface. Tap into the space where honesty lives in order to obtain a full and clear picture of what you really perceive)

- What are the honest perceptions of me that others hold?

  (Don't be afraid to ask those closest to you).

- Pertaining to the attributes I feel are displeasing about myself, what do I need to do to change them?

- Where am I in respect to where I would like to be?

- How far am I from manifesting the truth that is me?

- What steps can I take to get me closer to my envisioned self?

These are the same questions I asked myself after I got over my initial embarrassment. I wrote down my answers and pondered over them for a few days. It didn't take me much longer to finally make the decision to no longer make excuses. Since then, I have given my best effort to take action on all of my aspirations – big or small. I will be honest in saying I have yet to complete each and every endeavor. Still, I have made and continue to make great strides with my commitment to try. Through this small but significant shift in my outlook, I can honestly say that things in my very own life have enabled me to perceive success differently. So different, that I am compelled to share all that I've learned along the way with anyone in need of an influential shove to get them started on their own unique path and purpose. I am eager and more than willing to pass on to you the gift of support and inspiration.

So now that you are ready for change, make sure you stand tall and confident, grab hold of your courage as we prepare to zoom toward a galaxy of uncertainty, a universe of all possibility. As difficult as it may seem, try with all your might to jump out of your mind and into your spirit. That's it! Now, allow your spirit – your true self – to flow through your body freely. Embrace every ounce of your desire, every last one of your dreams and shout at the top of your lungs:

I am ready! I am ready! I am ready!

And now…

I give myself permission to achieve!

Here is a tip: If you are hesitant to scream these words from wherever you are standing; if you are reluctant to proudly share with the world your gifts, your purpose and your intentions; if you are actually more worried about what people might think of you than you are about expressing the willpower to change…it's quite possible that you are not ready for the success you are meant to attain. Consider whether you are more interested in entertaining the doubt, negative feelings and untruths that are perpetuated by fear and living from the perception of lack. Here is where you can take the time to determine whether or not you are more concerned with failing than you are with prevailing. Are you allowing the idea of what people may think of you if you don't quite "make it" keep you from taking an initial step from fear into freedom?

I hear the words of the infamous Dr. Phil ringing in my ear: "You wouldn't care what people thought of you if you really knew just how little they thought of you". This isn't saying you are insignificant in the worlds of your most cherished friends or even in those of strangers. What he is saying is, even if someone thinks you are crazy because you have the courage to do exactly what they fear and perceive to be abnormal or impossible, that person's judgment will be fleeting. Trust me, they will have their thought and go on about their day without hesitation. Encountering a "crazy woman" with big dreams and the audacity to scream her aspirations from the depths of her soul will have very little impact on that individual's life. Unless of course, they are open enough to receive inspiration to do the same.

That being said, throughout the days that lie ahead I want you to keep affirming those words above. Loudly, even if only in your mind. Let those words resonate so loud that your ears begin to ring. You do this, I can assure that you are in for a whirlwind of a life, crammed with fulfilled dreams and aspirations you once perceived to be unattainable.

Allow me, if you will, to share something else with you before we continue on to the first chapter. You see, being an athlete since the age of 10, I have always had a surplus of energy. It was (and still is) nothing for me to put all of my concentration and effort into any sports competition I've participated over the years, in all of which included swimming, softball, running races, and basketball (the latter lasting for a stretch of over 23 years). Never did I conceive of a day when my days of playing basketball would come to an end. Needless to say, that day finally arrived. I took up the seasonal game of tennis, which enabled me to exert much of the built up energy I had cruising through my body - consequent to the stresses that come with working, and building a dream. I even managed to maintain memberships at the local fitness centers, but my frequent workouts weren't quite enough to quell the urge to compete. That is, until I discovered an avenue leading me back to the game of basketball, through a newfound endeavor to become a D1 women's college basketball official.

The point is, in all of my creative ventures, success seemed disguised – at least in a financial sense. Eventually, I figured out that applying the same energies and exertions I had towards athletics into my aspirations, would bring me greater results in the area of dream realization.

Though I was never officially diagnosed with the condition, now that I have managed to gain greater insight, I believe that my short attention span and sporadic nature as a child could have been attributed to ADD. I am kidding when I say this, however, there is a little bit of truth in my contemplation. I am and have always been incredibly creative; my mind is constantly crammed with concepts, projects, business propositions, and ideas on how to "make the world a better place." One of the most frustrating things about "having so much energy" was that no sooner than I started one project or endeavor, I could just as quickly become enthusiastic about starting another. Very rarely did I get anything accomplished.

The good side to it was that, as a child I rarely suffered from boredom.

Unfortunately, my perception of being so active and flexible changed for me the moment I crossed the threshold of adulthood. No matter how resilient I may have been, I learned that life wasn't always so plain sailing; nor was it so willing to bend to my every desire without some sort of pay off. I came to the realization that I could no longer operate the same way I'd done as a child – moving from one interest to the next without building a solid foundation beneath my feet. Much like many others that I've had the opportunity to inspire or coach, I had no plan. Nonetheless, time was patient in allowing me to experience the natural evolution of me. By the time I reached my mid-twenties, I'd dibbled and dabbled in many things, but I was ill prepared for chaos that came with my ineptitude for focusing on one thing for a long period of time.

During one stage in my life (a short time before the "but" conversation with my friend) things went completely awry. The older I grew, the more experiences I accrued – some good, most substandard. The more enthusiastic about new projects I became, the longer my list of unfinished projects grew. The longer my list grew, the more I began to feel like a disappointment and a failure. The more of a failure I felt, the more insecure and uncertain in my abilities to succeed I became. All of this led me toward a downhill spiral of unpleasant experiences with people and situations that I allowed as a result of feeling undeserving of anything better.

I found myself standing alone in the middle of a shrinking room. The walls were beginning to cave in around me and I had no idea how I would ever escape the destruction of my crumbling world. I was literally dumbstruck, lost in utter confusion as I contemplated reasons as to why I'd suddenly glanced up and had nothing to show for the life I'd led thus far. ABSOLUTELY NOTHING. No degree, no kids, no family, no completed ventures, no successful television shows, not a single art exhibit or a single published book – nothing. This made no sense to me. After all, I'd spent years spinning my wheels trying to write the next best seller, trying to complete the next blockbuster hit, trying to start my own clothing line, trying to…I can go on and on with all of the things I tried and started, BUT, never finished. The ambition was there, but the plan was nowhere to be found.

Try as I might, I had absolutely no idea what happened and where it - failure - happened! Even worst, I had no idea where the time had gone. Suddenly, I couldn't breath. Anxiety gave its best shot at suffocating my mind with visions all of my failures. The fact that this sense of imprisonment had been created in my own mind didn't make this experience any more pleasurable. I'd done plenty of homework. I'd read every single self-help book I could possibly gather from every shelf, of every bookstore, I could find around the city. But, for some reason, my subconscious reaction to previous conditioning (environmental, emotional and spiritual) was much more powerful and controlling than the logic filled pages in the ever-growing pile of books sitting in the corner of my one-room studio apartment. Inertia had me nailed to the floor. Needless to say, that was the day I literally landed on my butt. I couldn't move. I sat there drowning in a sea of confusion without any idea how to let go of my "but" in order to swim towards the shores of freedom.

That was the same day I grew weary of the nothingness that was surrounding me like a dirty cloak. There was no way I could continue living my life in such a fashion. Something had to give. Somehow, someway, I mustered up enough courage to face the fears that were always waiting for me on the other sides of my "buts". As a result of my submission, I discovered the life I was meant to live and I haven't looked back sense. In hindsight, I now know that it is only through my not-so-pleasant experiences that I was able to acquire life's greatest lessons.

My sister, I share all of this with you to prove to you that I've been where you are. I understand what it feels like to reach the realization that your present state and circumstances don't match up with the images of success that you have in your mind. It is because I am enabled to look back into yesterday and tell you that I can relate to what you are going though. Thus, I feel it is my duty to do my best to grant you the keys to your freedom; keys that will also enable you to get off your "but", stand up and regain composure so that you too can go forth into the destiny you aspire to achieve.

As cliché and "happy-ending-ish" as this may sound, I assure you that today I live life striving to meet my greatest and highest potential and I desperately want to help you do the same. Whether or not it was/is my purpose to cross paths with you so that I might enlighten you with the gift of revelation that was once bestowed upon me, I can at least say that I could not have done so if I had never gotten off my "but" several years prior to this day. It is my hope that you remain open to learning how getting off your "but" can be the most rewarding decision you will ever make in your life.

Enjoy the journey!

Let Go of your But!

"The heart has its reasons of which reason knows nothing."

      -       Martin Luther

Let Go of your But!

Thinking Outside the Heart

*A*fter much consideration, I decided to incorporate this brief but vital chapter for one, very simple, yet, noteworthy reason. Every person – male or female – living and breathing on this great Earth yearns to cultivate two major areas in their lives: fostering relationships and reaching dreams. There is no way to escape these innate desires that we hold in the depths of our souls. There was a time where I, too, struggled with maintaining balance between love and happiness. I had a tendency to teeter recklessly and ineffectively between the objectives of finding passion in a partner or following my purpose. There have been many instances where I, unbeknownst to me at the moment, forfeited opportunities for progression on account of doing what I thought was the right thing for a relationship.

Please understand that this is not to say that love is irrelevant in the attainment of wholeness, however, I have reached the realization that relationships (even marriages) come and go. Wisdom has also taught me that just as crucial as finding a partner that suits my well-being is to my life, so is reaching fulfillment at my highest potential.

The problem is that some of us are clueless as to how to get the relationships we want while simultaneously putting the same amount – if not greater – of effort into bringing our dreams into reality. We have a tendency to allow our emotions about things or people to separate us from our authentic self. In our quest for love, we selflessly invite circumstances into our lives that are not in alignment with our true intention, without taking the time to listen for intuition's whisper. Thus, our feelings make it difficult for us to steer clear from events, places, people and things that can potentially break our hearts and destroy our lives (at worst).

When it comes to the matters of the heart, we as women often find ourselves somewhere in the middle of where or whom we want to be and the physical manifestation of that which we envision in our minds. Ladies, as displeasing as this may sound, I have to say this: we are often motivated to move towards our intended desires based upon whether or not our romantic relationships are failing or thriving. Let's be honest. If I asked you to reflect upon your journey up until this point, I am confident you will notice your most successful periods – or the least productive – were contingent upon whether or not you were in love, or devastated as a result of a very bad breakup or loss. I won't discount that there are a few who manage to accomplish goals while in a relationship, but nine times out of ten that will be a woman who is content with how the relationship with her mate has evolved. No offense, but this message is not for those few, but rather for the majority of us who have at some point chosen to settle for less than we deserve as a means of avoiding loneliness.

Let's face it, it really isn't until we feel we can do better that we get off of our "buts" and do something meaningful with our lives. This could range from losing weight, going to church, volunteering, practicing better parenting, etc. Usually, we don't think to do "better" in or with our lives until we become fed up with stagnation!!! Fed up with being walked on, overlooked, or taken for granted; fatigued by doing so much for others and seldom seeing kindness reciprocated. Most times, we do not feel compelled to change until we have had our heart shattered by someone we love; by someone we thought loved us. If you think about it, our greatest propensity to engage in self-reflection or contemplate necessary changes that will enable us to attract "something different" the next go 'round is when we are dealing with emotional chaos or tribulation. Does any of this sound familiar to you?

Please do not be distressed or feel ashamed by this truth. It is our nature to put others before us. We are nurtures, Mothers of life. We have been trained to say "yes." Yet we are frowned upon when "no" escapes our mouths. Selfishness is not our natural state of existence (emphasis on the word natural). Each and every one of us can retrace a path cluttered with tragedies and setbacks, disappointing memories and earth-shattering events to figure out exactly why we have yet to reach the point of achievement we desire and deserve.

Pay attention to this.

See where you could have done things differently and use them to make better future decisions when it comes to balancing your love life with your purpose driven life.

I'd like to take a second to speak, specifically, to single women who are in vehement pursuit of companionship. It is my intention to bring to your attention that, as women, you should apply the same amount of energy put into your quest for love into manifesting your dreams and goals. Also, understand that fearing the possibility of never finding the love you deserve, can be just as distracting as being in a relationship that does not serve you. In fact, entertaining thoughts about what you fear is actually, what keeps dreaded possibilities alive. As a woman, I recognize the discomfort that comes when fathoming the idea of going through life alone. Trust me, it gets harder as we grow nearer to our prime. Rounding the bend of mid-thirty and barreling head first towards my forties, I have reached a point where choosing to focus on the opportunities that come with being single, is far more rewarding than twiddling my thumbs, waiting idly for my knight in shining armor.

But every woman is different.

Choose as you must, but choose what works best for our life.

I'd be lying if I said it was easy. Yet, I realize that I am only equipped to make such a choice consequent to reflecting on a past, I painfully traversed while looking for love in all the wrong places. There is nothing worst than ending a relationship holding a bag of what feels like wasted time, thoughts and energy that should have been spent more wisely – as in on yourself. We are all very well aware of the "shoulda, coulda, woulda" feeling that comes when a season has ended.

Today, I am fortunately able to weigh the odds and do my best to control my emotions and fears in order to avoid making the same mistakes over and over, all for the sake of love.

If you are newly single, relish the endowment that comes with being with yourself. Do something different this time around. Self-actualization and goal attainment should now be your first priority; everything else – with the exception of children – is secondary. Still find harmony with your intentions, but put your authentic self first – even before you. Yes, you will struggle with ridding thoughts of a lonely, loveless future, especially with media running wild, with articles and news programming that speak to the ever-growing state of divorced and single women over the age of 35. I do, however, recommend that you refrain from allowing such visions to become your reality by giving it too much energy. After all, they are not naturally your thoughts, but rather thoughts that have been embedded through conversation with friends, family members and peers. You have the power to create your own reality. Hence, the reason you should quickly replace negative thoughts about relationships, by placing energy towards something creative and loving, all the while claiming that the Universe has something greater for you: something abundant, something beautiful and something better than your current state of existence. Fervently, believe that what is meant for you exists and hold fast to the desire to love a mate that is perfect for you. Until then, embrace your solitude, make the best of the gift of aloneness that some women do not have. Use the time to become the woman you envision in your future.

Getting back to the topic at hand, a disregarded but very important factor about engaging in and living a well-rounded life is finding harmony between our minds, bodies and spirits. Most of us are used to hearing the word balance when it comes to these three entities of our existence – of ourselves. I follow the mindset of the renowned spiritual author and life-coach, Dr. Rev. Iyanla Vanzant, who implies that "trying to find balance between our mind, body and spirit lives is setting us up for failure." I think we all can agree that it is extremely idealistic to think that portions of our lives will significantly outweigh another to the point of forfeit or sacrifice. That would entail putting 33.3% of our energy into cultivating our spirit, another 33.3% into stimulating our minds and another 33.3% into sustaining our bodies. In today's world, this is completely inconceivable. On the other hand, we can strive to discover and create ways to maintain an equal sense of gratification through the energies placed into pursuing our careers, seeking counsel or education, raising our children, staying active, going to church, entertaining ourselves, traveling…you get the point.

Iyanla says, "Harmony brings about a higher vibration than does finding balance. Remember that everything you do in your life gives energy and light to everything else you will do in your life." Meaning, everything you do – the energy you spend – today should move you forward in such a way that you are putting energy toward what you wish to occur later in your life. Remember, time is relevant to each circumstance. Put no limit on when "later" will arrive. This concept can be better explained through the words of Denzel Washington, in his role as a professor in The Great Debaters: "Do what you have to do, to do what you want to do." Or, as an acquaintance of mine, Melissa McGhie once said, "My whole objective in life is to be happy. I don't try to find equal balance in my work life, personal life and creative life…that's impossible. But, I can make sure nothing gets left out…and that's what makes me happy."

Here is a little point I'd like to bring to your attention. Most men are able to reach their successes much sooner than women, due to the innate ability to compartmentalize their lives and their ambitions; they are also able to focus on their endeavors more effectively because, unlike women, the matters of the heart do not drive them. Events or people who can potentially arouse emotions within them are less of a distraction. Consequently, men are better equipped at navigating in and out of the very things that provoke a sense of stagnation in the lives of women.

Maybe I have been presumptuous in assuming you are a woman who has yet to experience fruition in the realm of dreams and aspirations. Let's suppose that the majority of the women reading this book are looking for ways in which they can overcome obstacles that prevent them from living their purpose and sharing their true passion. However, there it is just as possible that this is not the case for you. In shifting our perspective, let's shoulder the possibility that your position differs in a sense that you have taken advantage of opportunities to climb every corporate ladder ascending into the heavens of executive leadership; maybe you are physically healthy, eating properly and getting the right amount of exercise conducive for improved well-being; maybe your financial portfolio is cushioned with stocks, bonds and assets you've worked hard at maturing; maybe you have raised your children and are ready to live a life where the focus of attention is on you. Perhaps, the only area in life where you have yet to garner positive and gratifying results is in the relationship department. Maybe, you are a woman who has reached a point where all you desire to attract into your life is a healthy, loving partnership.

Regardless of whether the portrayal of the woman I just described fits your make-up; or if you are a woman who is at the very beginning of her "thousand mile journey" into completion and fulfillment, consequent to having spent most of her time chasing love, the work to getting what you want is exactly the same.

What I am doing my best to illustrate in this chapter is that before you can move forward, you must get your mind and heart prepared to do the work it takes to think outside of your feelings; beyond emotional reactions to circumstances you don't prefer to experience; beyond the stories of victimization you feed yourself in order to justify discontent, inactivity, and scarcity. By now, it should be clear that the negative stories often entertained in your mind are very rarely factual, if ever. Fear not the deed of looking in the mirror and dispelling the truth of who you really are and what you really desire. It's the first step toward "letting go of the 'buts'" that hinder progress in your life. In my studies of Daoism (teachings and principles that disclose the art of living) over the years, I've learned a very practical philosophy that has helped me to completely modify the perceptions and paradigms I had about my own journey and the experiences I've encountered along the way. It says, "Clear your thoughts and end your problems." You see, regardless of the ordeals that have placed each of us upon this path towards fulfillment, each and every one of us has a history; a past that encompasses several pleasures, accomplishments, virtues and good deeds. However, there are the many faux pas, blunders, inadequate choices, and imperfections that take occupancy in a large part of our mental pantry. It is because of this compilation of life experiences that we continuously replay mental movies in our minds- that help shape and mold our perceptions about what may happen in our future. Most times we neglect to comprehend how viewing these illusions (remember they are neither real nor currently

35

happening) over and over contribute to "dream suicide". So by allowing these painful memories and disappointing occurrences of your past to recur in our minds, you essentially become the only person standing in your way. Remember, your thoughts about an incident or your emotional reaction to it can both serve as either a conduit for creating the world you so desire or a detriment to the act of giving birth to the dream dwelling inside you.

I tell all my friends "problems don't exist, but the negative thoughts that create them do." We, as women must begin to see ourselves through the eyes of our heart and spirit...not always the mind. Only then can we begin to alter sensitivities regarding our personal journey and current circumstances into constructive solutions that will. Therefore, we become equipped to eliminate 'problems' before they manifest, while at the same time, stay in alignment with our true intentions.

While you reflect on the inspiration above, consider the decree that says you have to be in the business of loving yourself enough to become and experience all that you were meant to carry out in your life. I will reiterate that fulfilling your purpose and your desired intentions, all of which lead to happiness, should then become the sole objective of your life. It is the only way in which joy will filter into all the other areas of your life. I recently read a quote from the Honorable Dalai Lama that stated: "The purpose of life is happiness". This statement can be used as a powerful tool in helping us navigate our way through life's daily problems. From that perspective, our task becomes one of discarding things that lead to suffering and accumulating the things that lead to happiness...When faced with feelings of stagnation and confusion, it may be helpful to simply reflect on what it is that truly brings us happiness, and then reset our priorities based on that.

Clear your thoughts... I urge you to stop playing emotional movies over and over in your head. Create new thoughts that bring about good feelings and contribute to you becoming the designer of your own outcome. This may be difficult while you are grappling through dark trenches of what feels like defeat, but it is very possible to accomplish. It just takes all of your effort.

...End your problems. Rid your mind of the tainted image that you hold of yourself as a result of your emotional reactions to the mistakes you've made or the disappointments of your past. Clear your pathway of obstacles and doubts so that you may move forward with clarity in order to focus on your intended goal. Swathe your mind with positive affirmations that provide you with the willpower and perseverance to stay the course until it reaches manifestation. Make deliberate choices in your thought patterns and the environment you keep. This may involve avoiding and expelling (temporarily or otherwise) yourself of people, places and events that cloud your heart and mind with disillusionment.

Your emotional harmony and your physical well-being will always be determined by the thoughts you hold in our mind. Any interference you experience as a result of your emotions – your heart – will definitely create obstruction in other areas of your life; that is, unless you do something about it NOW.

You must do the work, no matter how challenging things get. Be certain to check in continuously to see if you, your thoughts and the choice you make support your progression. Reflect over your past, but not long enough to get caught in the web of re-living your memories. Acknowledge your mistakes and accept who you have become thus far. Confront your fears. Partner your true potential with strength so that you may overcome anxiety and apprehension. Sometimes, you may be required to unlearn much of what you have learned, thus far, in order to move past the mental conditions that have kept you planted in place much longer than necessary. In this instance, no matter how difficult it is, I urge you to find the courage to take the pain – and/or joy in some cases – you feel inside your heart and use it as fuel to motivate you into moving into your next level of existence; to help you evolve in both your body and your spirit.

Again, the work will not be easy, but the outcome will be well worth the sacrifice. Just take the first steps!!!

Take the time to look at your current relationships. Evaluate their placement or contribution to your life and vice versa. Go a little deeper and observe the dynamics of your interaction with a lover, immediate family members, relatives, co-workers and friends. I guarantee there will be at least one individual in your circle that is the cause of some emotional clutter. At this juncture in your life, it is imperative that you confront the cause(s) for baggage, confusion or affliction you have accumulated as a result of its presence.

The point of this is not to place blame or dissuade you from accountability, but rather clear your path of obstacles that stand before you. Keep in mind that it is here, where you will decide whether you have the strength to adapt to the abhorrent situation, depending on whether or not you are ready for change or move away from the source(s) of grief and closer to your envisioned self. This doesn't necessarily mean that you need to remove yourself or change the situation in a harsh or painful way. If you feel that a person or environment is not supportive of your goals, simply tell the truth about it. This can easily be done in a way where you can avoid becoming the source of pain to someone else.

Relationships with other people should be helpful, not harmful. The aforementioned suggestion is not just a one-way street. I am a big advocate of accountability. People often forget that our lives are a direct reflection of our actions and thoughts. Needless to say, it wouldn't be fair if I didn't add this final note: It is healthy to consider whether or not you have a bad habit of inflicting pain onto others. The truth hurts, however, if you are the cause for the dysfunction in your relationship(s), you can also take the necessary steps of altering your mind patterns and outlooks, or even contemplate areas of change so that you become an imparter of love, joy, peace and well wishes for others.

Unless you take the time to ruminate over your actions (past or current), you may never become cognizant of the ill deeds or unkind words you tend to divulge. You may never understand how you perpetuate doubt and insecurity that prevents others from reaching their own dreams and aspirations. Just think…this kind of karma can also be the very issue that is keeping you from clearing your own consciousness and realizing your own aspirations.

Again, as a woman, it is your innate desire to nurture, to take care of others, and to act with compassion and empathy. The accumulation of wounds doled out by life's events may have inadvertently, become a wall of scarred tissue that envelopes what was once a very loving vessel. Understandable…Ask yourself this question: Do you want heartache to be the reason you neglect to carry out your life vision. Recognize that the thicker and thicker this wall grows, the more erosion begins to destroy the true gift that makes you a woman: your heart.

I am hopeful that you will be able to fully grasp the meaning of the following statement: Going against the current of your natural tendency to express compassion and observe benevolence in every one you come in contact with means that you have somehow created the habit of living through the ego. You have been experiencing life through the analytical mind that processes all of your negative encounters and hinders you from reaching out, exploring, as well as, attaining all you need to manifest the reality that is you. Instead of living through your spirit - your heart – you have allowed your ego to persuade you to utilize emotions, memories and intellect to guide you away from your purpose, rather than towards.

Being in constant awareness of your inner calling will aid in helping you to be mindful of the self-absorption in allowing your past experiences and future possibilities to keep you inactive; to keep you from living and connecting with others on an intimate level in order to bring you in proper alignment with all you are meant to have and fully bring into existence. What about you makes it okay for you NOT to flourish? What is so special that exempts you from trying to succeed? Who are you not to consider the potential for others to thrive as a result of being inspired by your presence? What purpose does emotional stagnation serve?

As long as you continue to brood over occurrences that either no longer exist or have yet to happen, you will never successfully create or attain the things you are meant to achieve.

"Hope and fear are both phantoms that arise from thinking of the self. When we don't see the self as self, what do we have to fear? See the world as yourself. Have faith in the way things are. Love the world as yourself; then you can care for all things."

These are words written by Lao Tzu, in a book of scriptures titled the Tao te Ching. It illustrates exactly how hope (a focus of energy placed on a future occurrence based on scarcity mindset entertained in the present moment) and fear (a focus of energy placed on potential failure consequent to an event that has already happened) are emotions generated through the contemplation of self and self only. Our smaller self – the ego – is always afraid of being pushed aside or discarded as a result of concentrating on and trusting in our Highest Self, our innate truths, our purpose, and our destiny. When we take the time to appreciate and embrace the present state of our reality – including who we are, removing the fear and hope of a future self can be very humbling. Thus, the space for creating and manifesting your deepest desires suddenly becomes available. You see, as long as your ego feels threatened it will always lead you towards finding ways to sustain itself. This usually comes in the forms of distractions, disease, discontent, discouragement and disappointments. The only way it can do this is to get you to focus on yourself, instead of seeing the world as the same true, egoless spirit that dwells at the center of your heart. It is the only way that you can clear the clutter of the past and move towards loving all aspects of you and those you encounter along the way.

Also, remember this: The very agony and trepidation you attempt to avoid by not changing your situation is actually locked inside of you, leaking toxicities that prevent you from being free to receive the abundance of resources and relationships that can help you on your journey to fulfillment. Just as the wall around your heart keeps people from getting in, it also hinders your true self from "being free" to evolve. As logical as it sounds or as secure as this may make you feel, you must realize that being in a constant state of defense takes you further and further away from your true intentions, your true purpose – your true spirit. The further way you drift from the image of self that you hold in your mind – consciously or subconsciously – the less capable you will be of connecting your present self with the self you envision.

There have been points in my own journey where I felt my life had been shattered as a result of bad judgment, poor choices or belief in people who I later discovered were unworthy of what I had to offer. Of course, I know understand that it was my own feelings of unworthiness that allowed me to be involved with such individuals in the first place. Now, because I have done, and continue to do, the work it takes to maintain emotional balance in my life, I can offer sound advice to women who experience the same types of challenges.

I have had many women come to me and share their fears of being alone. There have even been a few who have confided in me about their refusal to get too involved with someone for fear of losing herself in a relationship. Been there, done that as well. So, I understand what it means to recognize that who you are at this moment, is nowhere near the woman you desire to be. I am here to remind you: WE ARE NOT YOUR CIRCUMSTANCES. We are the spirit inside that whispers words of wisdom in our ear when we are out of alignment with our truth. Most times we do not listen. Other times we are too afraid to listen because changing our situation seems too overwhelming of an undertaking.

Here is what I say to that today: If you find that changing or freeing yourself from emotional turmoil – whether it is self-imposed or externally influenced – is too challenging, start small. Sometimes you can temporarily liberate yourself from an emotional crisis, heartbreak or disappointment by reminding yourself of the following: There is something out in the Universe that is much bigger than me. There is something the Creator has for me that is much bigger than this!

Turn your attention away from grief toward love.

Also, look at who you are in the lives of others. See your reflection in the faces of those who surround you and make the necessary changes. Adapting to change can be difficult. As it relates to relationships with other people in our lives we must accept the change of seasons, regardless of how bad or good the circumstances may have been. Wishing current or past conditions were different than what they turned out to be only leads to resentment and stagnation. Regardless of if you are single or not, determine if it's time to make some adjustments in your life and move forward. This could be a shift in your outlook so that you can start putting yourself first; begin walking in your highest potential. It could even entail leaving a relationship that is holding you back from your destiny. What matters most is that you remember to keep your vigor and forgive those who bring or have brought unnecessary destruction into your life. Preserve your power by recognizing they simply chose something opposite of what you preferred. Recognize that people are entitled to make their own choices, just as you are entitled to make the choice to grow, become and move beyond the pain and excuses.

"This is my simple religion. There is no need for temples; no need for complicated philosophy; our own mind, our own heart is our temple; the philosophy is kindness."

- 　　　　Dalai Lama

Let Go of your But!

Being Mindful of What You Are Really Sharing

*T*here is something to be said about an individual - male or female - who attempts to comprehend, respect, and honor the true meaning of marriage. Not only as it relates to a sheet of paper certifying matrimony between a husband and wife duo who have come into agreement to attempt living together as long as possible. But, also (or more importantly) as it is to be experienced beyond physicality; on a spiritual, emotional, physical and mental level that far transcends ordained traditions, keepsakes, photos albums, and wedding cakes.

Bear with me for a while (we will get back to buts in just a moment), and let's look further into the context of marriage, as we understand it in our culture:

1.   The legal or religious ceremony that formalizes the decision of two people to live as a married couple, including the accompanying social festivities: to officiate at a marriage. Synonyms: nuptials, marriage ceremony, wedding. Antonyms: divorce, annulment.

2.   Any close or intimate association or union: the marriage of words and music in a hit song. Synonyms: blend, merger, unity, oneness; alliance, confederation. Antonyms: separation, division, or disunion

Let us first delve into the concept of marriage as it is described in the first definition, being that it is the most common interpretation of the term used in our culture. Be it for the sake of being in love, embracing the idea of comfort that comes with having steady sex and companionship while still in good health, building a family, or simply growing old with another like-minded, or like-spirited being on this planet, the construct of marriage in today's society is nowhere near what it used to be. Without question, I am sure many of us can agree that the institution, itself, has evolved to a place where the "death do us part" declaration is seldom a commitment maintained through to completion. It's no secret that the rate of divorce today is at an alarming high. Yet on the other side of the coin, people are still buying wedding dresses and tuxedos, and going into debt to share one special day of bliss with each other in front of their friends and family. One has to wonder: Is matrimony really about promise and loyalty? Or is it just a social display of two people "trying to do the right thing" after a reasonable length of time; an attempt to avoid bringing a child into this world out of wedlock; or a justifiable explanation to silence the queries of elders regarding "offering your milk for free, without forcing him to buy the whole cow"?

Regardless of one's rationale, perception or judgment about the state of our marriages as a society today, we can at the very least acknowledge the gift that is shared when two people throw caution to the wind and traverse faithfully down an aisle with aspirations of making their lives stronger in union, harmony and affection.

Despite how a woman chooses to partner with her mate (marriage, no marriage, wedding, a trip to the courthouse, etc.), one horrifying belief she will most likely attempt to eradicate is one that perpetually implies that monogamy can be extremely challenging for most men. Though this thought pattern has been passed down from generation ("men are no good", "can't trust a man as far as you can see him", or "always keep a secret bank account, just in case..."), evidence of it seems to be increasing by the day. Thus, disloyalty is an unfortunate and heartbreaking experience, especially when we've exchanged vows, and expressed expectations, with hopes that all parties involved will uphold. What better way to prove one's highest intention of reverence and esteem for another. Right?

But what about vows and commitment we make to ourselves to maintain peace, joy, and fulfillment, by any means necessary? Some of us tend to forget about this innate covenant when it comes to following our hearts. We spend so much time and effort staying in situations that no longer serve us, while all the while neglecting to comprehend that the same quest for oneness we pursue with our mates or significant others, should be placed in our quest to experience completeness and contentment.

Then there is the implication that exclusivity goes against the biological nature; especially involving the male gender. On the other hand, some debate that the change in times (immediacy, accessibility and exposure to "extra-marital" opportunities) is the root cause for the rising divorce rate. We, as women, have to wonder whether or not things are really different than they were 50-years ago; an era in which our mothers were trained to turn the other cheek and pretend as though things within the relationship were copasetic, when they really weren't. Is it really harder to be monogamous today? Or, is it just easier to subject ourselves to being victimized by disloyalty consequent to the changes in times that make discretion much less challenging.

Now, how does any of this pertain to letting go of your buts?

Good question. Continue reading.

Here is the kicker Ladies. Regardless of whether or not you are a woman who is involved in a casual, intimate relationship or if you are married with intentions of creating the experience of having endless love, the true act of "marriage" occurs the moment two people make the choice to share bodies with one another. To go one step further, it is wise to recognize how your body parts themselves are merely tools through which your mind, emotion and spirit are conjoined with those belonging to another. There is no such thing as "casual" when you comprehend how you inadvertently accumulate "fingerprints" through the intimate sharing of yourself (and vice versa), as well as, how these "impressions" can largely affect your experience of the world and your relationships.

Until we are enlightened, many of us are far from mindful about the impact our choices in sexual partners and encounters contribute greatly to most of the anguish we suffer. Even when we manage to evade heartache resultant of separation or divorce, we are still connected to each and every individual with whom we have intimately engaged. Needless to say, we neglect to be accountable; to minimize our experience of pain by being much more selective about who we share emotional, mental, spiritual and energetic DNA with. In turn, we wind up being emotionally distracted and out of alignment with what is truly intended to unfold through our lives.

When we contemplate the exchange of energy that takes place when we are in our most vulnerable state, it's no wonder why some of us find farewell or dissolution of affairs excruciating. Any way you look at it, there is always an energetic meeting of minds and souls - however brief or lasting - whenever you decide to offer yourself to another while in your most exposed, uninhibited state of being. The thoughts and energies that are shared during the process of what is proposed for creation (not just in a reproductive function, but rather also including the overall desired experience of connection) is something you may devalue. Creative power is a force to be reckoned with; yet, we as women take it for granted for the sake of momentary pleasure. How you honor and/or dispense your creative influence within your intimate life, most likely plays out in an identical fashion in other areas of your life.

Ask yourself:

1. Do I misuse or abuse my power (sexually or otherwise)?

2. Do I allow other people to devalue or underestimate my

sense of authority?

3. Do I give my authority away wastefully, and then blame others for victimizing me?

4. Do I withhold and limit my sharing contingent upon what someone else does for me?

What does this have to do with success or fulfillment?

Keep reading.

I write this chapter as an homage to all my sisters, not to condemn, judge or even conspire with you in your belief – and rightly so, considering how far along this difficult journey we have traversed, to get to this present moment within a male-dominated culture – that now is your time to go for what you want in life. Be it in relationships, sexual encounters, business, careers, etc., the life you aspire to live always starts with today – not yesterday, and not tomorrow. This includes modifying your choices and aligning them to ones that are more conducive to your emotional, physical, spiritual and intellectual well-being.

For so many years, the subject of sex has been a taboo topic and rarely a conversation shared between women, daughters and our female siblings. For so long we have entertained beliefs and conditions about relationships with men and sex, that were not necessarily our own, but rather inherited from preceding generations. Some of these principles and philosophies worked well for the time and period in which they were shaped, but they have now become antiquated. These principles take our focus off being accountable and force us to find blame on the actions of others. The idea of keeping the subject of sex, including the repercussions of choosing inadequate partners, no longer stands in alignment with the intention to carry out our lives in truth and fullness. Cultivating and respecting the Feminine Divine Nature within, is a necessary choice in discovering and experiencing the innate happiness we became heir to the day we came into existence.

In my attempt to guide you towards accountability so that you can consciously choose to minimize pain, and/or suffering you may encounter in your life, learn how to love yourself for who you really are, not for what you have anatomically. Remember, pain is inevitable, but suffering is optional. Judging, conspiring, or comparing our relational experiences with one another doesn't help matters either. Instead, empowering each other to make better choices and decisions about whom we partner with – not just physically, but emotionally, spiritually and mentally as well – is essential to curtailing the discomfort of moving forward after a relationship has reached its season's end.

Preachy is never my selection of impartation, however, I would like take this opportunity to remind you of your divinity. Your body is your temple; one that should be devoutly cherished. I invite you, if you haven't already done so, to grow more heedful as to who and how you allow someone to "worship" within, outside and around the shrine that has been bestowed unto you. You can begin by shifting your perception of physical intimacy as a means of connecting (becoming one with; marriage) and creating harmony, instead of a conduit for manipulation and harm. Instead of using sex as a diversion from having to confront the chaos, confliction, and confusion of your past, find a way to perceive it as a priceless practice that allows you – and others – to get to know yourself more personally.

From this moment forward, you can begin recognizing opportunities to be more mindful and responsible for the karma, harmony and balance you draw into or repel from your life experience. Expand your consciousness for a moment and begin to contemplate what your intimate experiences would be like – including how it infects, effects and affects yourself or another person – if you were to perceive sex as a form of meditation; a space where you and your partner could be more open and available to one another; a universe where oneness, creativity, intimacy and complete attunement and presence can be mastered.

Genitals are actually unessential in the moment of sharing and exchanging our true self with someone we are attracted to, love and adore. This being the case, one's sexual preference neither enhances nor alters the experience of relating on energetic, emotional and spiritual levels. Whether we choose to acknowledge and act in accordance to it or not, sex is a spiritual act – not as in a religious ritual, but rather pertaining to the act of creating something that can be perceived as enjoyable, beautiful and fulfilling in the present moment, the only moment we truly have. It is in the midst of exchange where we are able to dance, celebrate and share without inhibition; where surrender, faith and trust are practiced naturally.

This can sometimes be a scary and unfathomable experience for women, especially those who have survived incest, rape or molestation. This is why it is very important to recognize how knowing yourself, cherishing your temple and honoring your feminine sacredness is extremely significant in how you unfold, perceive and experience things that occur in your life. The moment you can recognize that the beautiful woman residing in your core, buried beneath all the suffering, all the scars, the wounds and the infliction...the moment you can start to liberate yourself from pain and limitation, you can begin to healthily and fearlessly allow someone to bring to the surface what you innately desire to experience from within.

Here is something else you can consider while on this journey to fulfillment. Recognize where you tend to be inert in your life, sitting around waiting on the "right" situation, the "right" person or the "right" circumstances (finances, career, stability, etc.) so that you can share intimacy with your "knight in shining armor". You call yourself being selective about with whom you share romantic feelings, deep connection and passionate encounters. You wait, and wait, and wait... When not careful, the quest for infatuation and romance consumes you to the point of inaction and stagnation. You spend much of your time waiting on the arrival and presence of what feels genuine based on what someone else appears to be doing or not doing.

What you as a woman may be failing to understand is that people do not bring anything to you in intimate situations. An individual cannot make you feel sexy, attractive, vulnerable, and connected. Instead, people bring out of you what is already there. All of your stories, thoughts, beliefs, and conditions about yourself, and people or circumstances in general (true or otherwise), are suspended the moment you allow the state of surrender and vulnerability become you. They simply cease to exist. It is then this state that the authentic, highest self - our most desired, sensual self – thrives, in all of her wonder and beauty. The more you experience her, the more you will be willing to share her with others, in a way that is conducive to her, and your, well-being. The more you are able to share your true self with others, the more empowered you become in liberating yourself in other areas of your life. Respecting and honoring you, while at the same time letting go of your fear of being alone, will clear up the space within that will enable you to attract like-beings into your life.

Life gets better when we are able to mindfully express ourselves in a way that is healing, loving, compassionate and pleasurable, and ultimately leads to happiness. Being conscious of how and who we share our bodies with is one of the most effective ways to do this. Why? Because according to Deepok Chopra, "bliss, carefreeness and playfulness are the essence of sex and intimacy. In sex, as in all areas of life, resistance is born of fear. All resistance is mental. It implies judgment against what is being felt. Sex becomes a problem when it gets mixed with hidden emotions such as shame, guilt and anger."

What exactly does this mean, Ladies?

It means that any inhibitions, fears or limitations we have regarding being intimate with another person has everything to do with how we feel about ourselves. Remember, the only true relationship/experience we are ever truly having is the one we have with self. This insight alone can help you bring focus to your relationships as it relates to letting go of your buts, and the hindrances that prohibit success, achievement and fulfillment. All of which provides opportunity for increased awareness and accountability.

On another note, beware that of all the intentions to be attained through the coming together of two people (sex, love, romance, financial increase, friendship, business, etc.), commonality isn't enough to sustain storms, trials and tribulation. A collective purpose, mindset, meaning or the types of choices and decisions made (individually or mutually) throughout your journey together. Resolution or situational assessment in any relationship should be embraced or rejected according to how they can potentially affect the overall purpose of your union. This means that, at the very least, one should practice choosing to be in the presence of someone who aspires to help you get better and better, while at the same time aiming to reach their own potential – even in a sexual capacity. With this in mind, you should begin to become heedful of the people you allow into your circle, your environment, your emotional space and your body. From this moment forward, begin to consider whether or not a person is in alignment with your overall life purpose; whether or not he or she contributes the life experience YOU envision creating.

This is how being selfish, or encountering the toxic deeds of self-centered individuals can be avoided. As long as your purpose stays in the foreground of your mind, without getting lost in the disillusion of lust, infatuation, appeal or increase, you will never be content with dishonoring self or allowing others to dishonor you. Thus, it is wise to start placing significance on serenity, peace, gratification, joy and fulfillment, especially in the event you are involved in a troubled relationship. Otherwise, you will continue along a path leading you away from your intended experience.

Relationship (intimate, or otherwise) breakups or break downs have very little to do with one's level of interest. Realistically, it's the change in common interest, the dissimilar levels of growth, and the ability to make choices and decisions founded on mutually respected principles, values and intentions that causes a relationship to diminish or reach its demise.

"You are what your deep driving desire is. As your desire is, so is your will. As your will is, so is your deed... As so is your deed, so is your destiny."

- Brihadaranyaka

Let Go of your But!

Dream Discovery and Disclosure

*R*emember, in your quest to seek balance and harmony in your life (both of which are essential to clearing the space for cultivating a more successful and fulfilling experience), the intelligent choice would be to always consider where correction or change about a particular condition, perception, pattern, behavior or belief could be implemented on at least two of the four levels of your existence: mental, spiritual, physical and emotional. In the previous chapter, I am hoping you have become more aware of the growth and modification that can be experienced on the emotional, physical and spiritual levels.

We can both agree that seeds of inspiration and intention are planted in the garden of imagination - the mind. This of course means that the manifestation of your highest ambitions is facilitated through your mental realm.

Taking heed to the above statements, maybe you can begin to understand why it is imperative to ponder feasible ways to share your goals and objectives. If you are not vigilant about what and how you share what has been rooted in our mind, just like with your body, you could potentially fuse your elation and excitement - about life, a future aspiration, a business venture, or whatever you intend to create within your now moment - with individuals who may hold energies that are unsupportive or obstructive. Of course, this can serve to be counterproductive, yet we all have been guilty of being oblivious and insensible about with whom we engage in conversation. By all means, I am in no way saying get rid of your "non-supportive, coy or disbelieving" friends, but rather be a tad bit more selective about what you share with whom. This doesn't even mean you should alienate yourself from your circle of beloved girlfriends who may not share the same passion for accomplishment and gratification. However, consider just how many of the people who surround you actually lend support for your vision. Who around you would go to the moon and back just to ensure you make it to the reality side of your dreams? How many of your friends and acquaintances project onto you dreadful queries filled with their own doubt and inability to see beyond their own circumstances?

Truth of the matter is, your life is your life…your vision is your vision…your passion is your passion. So to expect other people to be 100 percent on board with you and your journey into self-actualization is futile. To do so, is to be disappointed 95 percent of the time. On the other hand, there are the needles in the haystacks that have the capacity to supersede the usual propensity to "hate", judge, doubt, complain, and give you every reason in the book why whatever you are pursuing "will never work."

Hence, the reason it is wise to recognize who stands with and for you in support of your dreams. Just the same, feel compelled to determine which of your friends, family members, relatives or co-workers are constantly playing the role of pessimistic realist, devil's advocate or the cynical critic. When you are able to weed out those who do not share the same frequency or vibration as your truth, you can avoid getting caught in a marsh of negativity or blockage that inadvertently hinders your flow into fruition. Or…you may just as well discover the benefits that come with being powerfully charged and supported by those rare few who are dialed into the same current of inventiveness and resourcefulness as you.

Try it.

I guarantee you will discover how maintaining your selectivity about revealing your aspirations through the ritual of conversation can have a great impact on how things transpire in your life.

Here is how I came into such insight:

In my early years (long before I was aware of what it really meant to be mindful), I crossed path with an owner of a small talent management company who recognized my aptitude as a budding artist. Riding the heels of possibility, she proposed the pursuit of creating opportunities from which we could both benefit monetarily, consequent to exposure for my talent. Her first objective was to take advantage of her connections in the music industry in order to crystalize my lofty yearning to design album covers for some of the local groups, who were also looking for exposure. Her only request was that she received twenty-percent commission for every job she acquired. The wage seemed rather high, yet my exhilaration of the moment propelled me hastily past my own apprehension.

To say I was excited is a severe understatement.

After proudly collecting my compensation for the first assignment (an illustration for a then rising R&B singer, Gerald Alston), I was instructed by my newfound manager to be very careful about sharing my success with others. "You can't go around telling everyone what you are doing, because if you do…nothing you speak will come true. The devil will make certain to take it from you," she warned.

Initially, my first thoughts were to ignore the ridiculousness of her prophecy. Why would I not want to share my success? No one I knew had an opportunity to design album covers for some of the local music acts. This was an achievement – not just for me, but for all of my creative friends. In fact, this was something I'd dreamed about fulfilling since I was a junior in high school. Perplexed and confused about my manager's intuition, I went as far as to call an associate of mine to see what she thought about the suggestion. She conspired, "That's what she believes. You don't have to believe that stupidity." I could hear her sucking her teeth on the other end of the phone. "Just say, 'uh huh' and get paid. In fact, her asking for twenty-percent of all your hard work is hilarious. I suggest you tell her ten is more like it."

I called that support back then.

What...? I was twenty-two. How was I to know my "friend" was guilty of pouring a toxic elixir into my punch bowl of dreams? How could I have been aware of the fact that an opportunity such as this usually only came once in a life time? How could I have possibly known that twenty-percent was a standard commission rate for managers? More importantly, why couldn't I see then that this woman knew more than both me and my friend put together, and that she probably had great reason for sharing her thoughts?

Needless to say, I never came into agreement with my manager's proclamation; at least not consciously. Unfortunately, our business arrangement ended the moment I counter-proposed a ten-percent commission, which apparently offended her to the utmost degree. In hindsight I am able to see how a small, tiny part of me intuitively feared her words to be true, especially since our brief endeavor ended so abruptly after having shared my opportunity with an acquaintance. Today, I still carry that disastrous learning experience, and I can't say that I ever fully recovered.

Ironically, there came a point somewhere in my journey where I began to recognize that anything that I envisioned or scribbled into my dream/goal journal somehow came to fruition. However, anything that I expressed verbally seldom moved beyond the realm of my mind's eye. I began to notice after excitedly sharing with friends my intentions for creating projects, collaborating with others to build reliable resources, developing business ideas or pursuing ventures that would elevate me as a wise and creative individual; how it seemed as though these intentions fizzled shortly after my disclosure. It wasn't as if one or two, or even three ideas that I'd mentioned to other people came and past without so much as peaking its head into the physical realm of reality. No...my awareness of this experience revealed that about 90 percent of all things about which I'd spoken, without writing them down, failed to reach completion.

Recently, after years and years of frustration, I had begun to wonder whether I'd been cursed by my manager's words (I mean this humorously), or if there was some actual truth to what she'd advised. Being that I have long since stopped focusing my attention on to what most refer as the devil (other than respecting the universal law of polarity that says there is an opposite to all things, including goodness), I resisted the possibility that there was something in the spiritual realm that could actually snatch something from its path toward realization. I soon realized that my confusion about this reality had me compelled to seek consultation and guidance. There was no way I was willing to settle any longer for such a simple reasoning that did not fall into alignment with anything I believed.

A dear acquaintance of mine, who deems herself a Prayer Warrior, happened to be on the phone with me when the peculiarity of my realization came to mind. Reluctant about conceding to the possibility of sounding preposterous, I shared my bewilderment with the soon to be source of enlightenment.

But not so quickly did I reach such illumination...

Once I felt complete with my sharing, I was met with more mystification when I was plainly advised "to be more mindful of how and with whom you reveal your aspirations...to stop having conversations with everyone about what you intend for your life." I understood what she was saying, but clearly she'd misunderstood my request for resolution. So, slowly and patiently, I restated my confusion. And she kindly repeated: "There is some truth to what that lady told you...not entirely, but mostly. All in all, change your focus from the intentions behind her words. Instead, practice being more mindful of how and with whom you share your aspirations...stop having conversations with everyone about what you intend for your life. Not everyone can handle and/or support the magnitude of the responsibility you have to live up to your vision without envy, fear, judgment or doubt."

In fact, the profundity of her statement hit home in a resounding way. But, it did nothing to quiet my confusion.

"But," I started, utterly muddled, "Isn't this about me…not them…not the people with which I am sharing?"

For the life of me, I could not see, hear or understand why in the world she was advising me to point my attention outwardly; rather than guiding me toward finding some - condition within me that apparently needed healing or breaking. I figured that they - other people - had nothing at all to do with the fact that I seemed to be silently and unconsciously entertaining what was beginning to feel like a curse. So to place focus on what wasn't transpiring for me onto an external source didn't make sense to me. This too seemed extremely counterproductive.

A few days later, the insight behind my lesson finally revealed itself:

You can make aspirations and desires more powerful when deliberately expressed or shared with people who are not already listening to the doubts and disbeliefs they may have of themselves and of you. Unite in conversation with people who can hold your thoughts, aspirations, goals and desires in the highest form of vibration, affirmation and purpose.

Ahh Haaaa!! So powerful, isn't it?

Never once had I considered the limitation and destruction I had been causing in the unfolding of myself and my dreams through the careless sharing of intentions.

So as a result of this exchange, I offer the same insight to you. Now…in this moment, I encourage you to imagine what your life would look like if you were more mindful about whose energy you are merging with your verbal expression of an aspiration, goal or intention. Consider your circle of friends. Write them all down on a list and grade each one according to the level of support or opposition they have contributed to your life. The objective is not to judge, but rather bring to your awareness your energetic partnership with what you desire to manifest in your life. From this list you can better determine which of those individuals are more likely to stand in full espousal – through prayer, promotion, provision, etc. - of your dreams.

Let Go of your But!

"Truth at times can be either unbearable or supportive, depending on where we are on our journey back to self. It is in our ability to adapt to change that truth can also serve as the blade that carves away layers of scabs that hide who we really are at the core of our being."

-Kimberly E. Banks

Let Go of your But!

The Moment of Truth

*T*here should be no offense taken in the assumption that you are reading this book as a result of realizing and recognizing you are in a state of sluggishness or a state of existence that you perceive difficult to escape. This being the case, let's point attention to the reality that there are many people in this world who – in a moment of truth – find themselves standing in what feels like a pit of quicksand, unable to move from point A to point B. So treasure comfort in knowing you are not alone. While we are at it, take a moment to get a more in depth glimpse over the years you have lived up until now. For the simple fact that you have arrived at the point where you require inspiration in order to reach the tangible side of your dreams, I imagine that you are probably experiencing some sort of innate tug on your life that you haven't figured out how to pursue.

Recognize and understand the power of ingenuity you have dwelling within.

It is to the degree you are able to distinguish your own ability to move past stagnation, inertia, fear and sentiments of unworthiness – all of which are supported by the multitude of excuses you invite into your mind – through creativity and imagination, is the degree in which you will be empowered to manifest exactly what you desire to experience in any given moment. In this understanding, circumstances do not matter. Relationships are not hindrances. Environments are not limiting. Success in your job or career path is not stalled. From this perspective, it is easy to come into the awareness that it is ONLY your thoughts and beliefs that prohibit you from experiencing much needed changes, desired outcomes, fulfillment and the attainment of aspirations in your life.

Contrasting practices and levels of productivity, as it pertains to what you truly desire and prefer, are meant to point your attention back toward the pool of deliberate intention where all things are new, yet conceivable and attainable. Here is where focusing energies on possibility – or its opposite - plays a significant part in what and how things transpire along your path.

Today is the day you begin to create new ideas, new concepts, new thoughts and new beliefs about yourself and what is occurring in your world.

But for now, if you are in tune, as well as, aligned with the life you desire to live, you may be feeling a sense of purpose with which you can't quite connect, but are certain exists. Or, perhaps you were born with a gift that can potentially make you a millionaire or may possibly enhance the lives of thousands of people around the world. I bet with further speculation, you'd discover a knack for writing, teaching, creating, singing or cooking. Is it possible that you have a monumental idea nestled deep inside you that has remained dormant for years, just waiting for you to seize the "right" opportunity to bring it to fruition? Yet, isn't it apparent by now that your great opportunity won't come knocking on your door. Isn't it obvious you have the power to create it?

Here is a reminder: Without you, your life cannot happen.

Digging further, I am almost certain you are a woman with children, a family, friends, and a job – all of which take up so much of your time, you can barely fathom being anything else but a worker bee, mother, wife, or daughter. Possibly, you are in a relationship that makes you feel sad, lonely or anything other than the love, romance and adoration for which you so deeply yearn. Or, like many women striving to get ahead, you are nowhere close to being financially stable enough to endeavor the achievement you know you are meant to attain.

So there we have it...the big picture. All of the above are some very understandable reasons as to why you may still be holding onto your "but," waiting for a miracle to materialize. As harsh as this may sound, are you prepared to take heed to the notion that the only true reason you are unable to muster the energy, strength, finances, time or courage it takes to let go of your excuses and craft the life you desire is - you. The only person, impediment or challenge keeping you from ensuing success and fulfillment is you and your thoughts!!!

There is only one person responsible for your life.

There is only one person equipped to take steps toward dream fruition in your life.

That person is you and ONLY you!

You are on a one-woman act designated to bring down the house and command an encore. You are the captain of the Dream Team, who is completely reliant upon you to bring home the championship trophy. Thus, it is imperative for you get off the sidelines and become an active participant in the game you chose to play. Life is depending on you to carry out the role you intended to live the day you entered this world. More importantly, the time has come for you to expand in consciousness and recognize that you are merely a small part of a bigger picture that makes up this the world, this universe.

Whether you like it or not, you are a contribution to something larger than yourself. It's up to you to determine how you will do so: unfavorably or auspiciously.

Either way...it's your choice. Just don't let us down.

It isn't until you can see how large of a part you play in the unfolding of your life's events that you will instigate responsibility for your entire life – the good, the bad, the failures, and the successes. Until you can accept all that has happened up until today, as well as, acknowledge the work you need to complete in order to reach your next level, it is impossible to attain a clearer perspective as to how to go about reaching your greatest aspirations.

For a second, just imagine what your life would look like by now if you had already been accountable for your own destiny. What could you have accomplished before this time if you hadn't been waiting around on others to approve of your innermost desires? How free would you be now had you taken ownership of the proverbial paintbrush and designed your own masterpiece of life? What if you hadn't been waiting around on someone else – your mother, spouse, child, boss, friends, etc. – to give you permission to achieve your dreams?

Take a moment to visualize where you could be, where you could go, right now if you weren't swimming inside an ocean of excuses and negative beliefs that only exist between your ears.

Don't worry. All is not lost. It is NEVER too late to bring your treasure chest filled with "coulda, shoulda' woulda's" out of retirement.

Here is something to consider as you dust off your Pandora's box of excuses. Ask yourself, what could your life look like, right now, if money and fear were not an issue? Now, would you believe me if I told you that you have access to the same resources utilized by the likes of Bill Gates, Oprah Winfrey, or Donald Trump?

Well you do. It's called your mind.

Inside your mind is where trust, faith, belief, creativity, imagination, focus and intention come together to institute the awakening of your greatest potential. The difference between you and a renowned music mogul, best-selling author, inventor, entrepreneur or philanthropist is not wealth. It isn't charm or personality. It isn't talent. It isn't a network of associates or "people" who are connected, respected and cherished by persons in their industry. Truthfully, there is really only one thing that differentiates you from the successful individuals you esteem. The variance lies in how you choose to harness your unique and imaginative power. Of course this entails your ability to stay the course, remain focused, hone your gifts and commit to completion and fruition. However, being that every single person on this planet is designed to succeed (no matter what our circumstances may dictate), choice remains to be the only obstacle standing between you and the life you desire.

As you muse over this insight, slightly shift your perspective from your current circumstances and begin picturing yourself living as though you have already achieved your biggest dreams. Allow your imagination to connect you with the feelings, sounds, security, peace of mind and state of being you will experience the day you are able to reflect over your journey to success and fulfillment. Recognize the mountains of "buts" and excuses you had to surmount along the way in order to reach your destination. Sense the ambition, the tenacity, the love, the passion and the desire that moved you forward. Envision yourself prevailing through resistances and challenges while keeping your eyes, ears, and heart focused on realizing your truth, your purpose and your dream.

Remember "the journey of a thousand miles starts right beneath your feet." This means that in order to get what you want out of life you must first accept where you are now, and how far you have come, without regret, judgment or comparison. The exercise above is meant to show you what is possible when you take ownership of your destiny. If it isn't clear to you yet, give it a few more seconds. Once you have that picture in your head, the questions you should then ask are:

1. How do I get from my present circumstances to my desired reality?

2. Where do I begin?

3. Is time or age a relevant factor in whether or not I can \ attain success?

4. If so, how can I get from point A to point B in the shortest time possible?

5. What resources do I have within me? What resources surround me?

6. Who can support me in this endeavor?

7.

Contemplating tactics on how to scale what may appear to be an insuperable wall can be difficult initially, especially, if it is void of the necessary footholds to help you ascend. The distraction of difficulty, itself, is often times hard for some of us to purge. Even once we begin fathoming the idea of possibly making the first risky reach for a mere indentation in the wall, our head is instantaneously clouded with thoughts of: What if I can't finish? What if I am not strong enough? What if I fall? Who will call the ambulance when I do? Will the ambulance be able to get to me on time? What if the ambulance has an accident driving at breakneck speed just to get to me??!!

Absurd…I know. But, you would be surprised at how easily our ego can distract us from our objective when permitted. The hypothetical situations running in our head can potentially go on and on if we allow our mind to become convoluted with nonsensical thoughts. Usually, it's the first question, the initial diversion from reality that has us defeated before we even get started. One superfluous question can lead us onto a path of disruption, taking our attention away from what we set out to accomplish in the first place. In the example above, observe how the first "what if" is just as irrelevant as contemplating the possibility of the "ambulance getting into an accident" on the way to rescue. As soon as a negative "what if" enters our mind, we should try our best to extinguish it and focus on the task at hand.

Here is another fascinating point to deliberate: There are many times in our pursuit of success where tunnel vision (an extreme sense of focus) can inadvertently obstruct our view of potential opportunities that lie outside the realm of what we deem possible. We have a tendency to look for opportunity in the places we have already ventured. Instead of taking a step away from impediments that stand before us, thus getting a wider glimpse of the entire view, our main focus became "the wall's" aesthetics – its height, width and length, along with the elements with which it was constructed, so on and so on. While caught in distraction (or focus, depending on where our attention is placed), we are oftentimes oblivious to the door (exit or entrance) positioned smack dab in its center. There it stands, waiting; extending an open invitation to all who have the wherewithal to distinguish it, even if camouflaged. Yet, in our blindness we miss the opportunity to "walk through" our challenge.

Of course, this is all a metaphor relating to the challenges and obstacles we encounter on a daily basis. Yet, we should still be inspired to take a step back and get a clear understanding before you proceed with our endeavor to overcome. Whether it is positioned at the center of your "but" or at the center of your spirit, resolution is always available. Taking the time for discovery helps to douse our fears and interferences with confidence that comes through the attainment of knowledge and wisdom, which ultimately comes as a result of experience.

Solutions can only come if you believe they exist. Resolutions arise the moment you tap into the same Energy,

Belief or Possibility that gave you Life; that placed the seeds of aspiration and inspiration in the core of your heart before you were even born. Having the patience and courage to realize your true purpose will always lead you towards opportunities to actualize whatever you deem possible. With this in mind, you'll be enabled to breakthrough anything that has hindered you from accomplishing your goals. On the other hand, these same opportunities and possibilities are forfeited the moment you start focusing your attention on the negative aspects of any situation.

I have never heard of anyone consumed with doubt succeeding, but I have seen dynamic things happen to people who allow their inner spirit to be drenched by faith. Pastor T.D. Jakes once said, "Believing hurts...believing will cause you to give your all and see nothing in return...but believing also gives you the strength to continue despite your adversity."

I have an amusing view about the concept of faith that continues to arouse debate among my peers. Here is what I have come to learn: We all know that "leaping into faith" is one of the primary steps necessary for making our way toward achievement, success, or fulfillment. However, if we are not mindful, the faith into which we leap can eventually serve as a permanent holding place for our deepest aspirations. We sometimes have a tendency to let go of our aspirations and offer all of our allegiance to what's "meant to be," without ever engaging in actions that support the fruition of what we desire. There comes a point where we must relinquish the need to hold on to our faith (speaking in reference to the truism that most of us profess when a loved one faces challenges) so that we can position ourselves to make the prevailing rise from faith and travel into the experiential side of our aspirations.

Sometimes you must wear the jersey while holding both the diagramed clipboard and playbook – this makes you the player, the captain and the coach – when playing it big in the game of life. You must learn to creatively devise masterful strategies, bring the ball up the court, and manage the players on your team, all at the same time. Sometimes it's the only way to win the game. There won't always be someone cheering you on from the sidelines, telling you who to guard, where to go and what play to run. There will be many times where the only person encouraging you to prevail, find resilience, or re-affirm your commitment to victory is YOU. During these periods, you will be the only person dependable enough to help you replenish your tenacity and rearrange your line of attack.

Most people operate with the mindset of doubt, or fearful "what if's" when it comes to living out the life to which they aspire. Practice doing the work it takes to change your thoughts and it is inevitable that you will be moved to change your actions, which will ultimately change your conditions. Getting to the other side of your desired intention may involve making a few modifications in your thought process. However, you can do it! For starters, the words "I can't" must be completely removed from your vocabulary; and second, it is vital that you make a promise to do away with wasting time talking yourself out of moving forward. NOW is the time you begin deliberating powerful thoughts that propel you head first into the wonderful world of success, fulfillment and imagination. Your time is precious. Putting off what you can do today until tomorrow is not the mark of a successful person. Don't be a procrastinator another moment longer.

Remember: This is your dream, your future and your life.

Today is the day the path to your future changes! It's the day you succumb to that fervent urge inside of you that has been trying to boost you to do more with your life. There is a gift, a talent, and a purpose that no one else but you have been put here on this Earth to do. NOW is the time you begin to recognize who you are, what your capabilities are, and how valuable you are to the whole scheme of the world in which you live.

Through the life you live, you have a compelling opportunity to contribute to your existence, other's existence, and the transformation of humanity as a whole. That is a huge responsibility, but an even bigger gift when perceived through the essence of compassion and creation. Here is where you acquaint yourself with the notion that eventually everything you offer to others, via your unique attributes, will ultimately lend great value to the world as a whole. You do this by being of service to others whose journeys and experiences are heightened as a result of your presence; through the gifts, talents and passions that have been bestowed unto you. Think of the ripple of energetic vibration, the domino effect that can occur through the people you touch, inspire, teach or empower to make the same commitment in their lives, and so on and so on.

As stated earlier, such utterances as "I can't" will no longer be emitted from your mouth. From this point forward, you will begin to say, "I can do all things…no matter how hard it is or how long it takes!" It is time for you to tap into your potential and muster all that is necessary to move you towards your dream.

Let's briefly talk about purpose.

Whether or not we ever stumble across the great epiphany that explains the meaning of life, we all are born with a purpose for which we have been specifically chosen to fulfill. You must be open to the understanding that your purpose may very well be for the sake of your own individual contentment; or you just may have an assignment that has been divinely designed for the sake of enlightening, impacting, sharing, and inspiring millions of people around the globe. I am inspired to share with you what one of my most esteemed mentors imparted unto me at the beginning of my journey to realization and achievement: Life is not a process of discovery that we are meant to master over a period of years. Life is a process of creation – be it deliberate or accidental. Each moment, situation or opportunity that arises presents to us a chance to change who we are in order to become who we aspire to be.

Beloved, I invite you to take the time to discover some of the unique attributes you possess that can essentially be used to enhance your work experience, empower yourself to be of uninhibited service to others, or possibly turn a much cherished hobby into a viable business.

What are you good at?

What is that one thing you would do even if nobody paid you a single cent to do it?

If, and when, you can answer those two questions, devote yourself to finding a way to use your gifts and talents, and to ultimately lend a helping hand in the upliftment and unfolding of others in their journey to success.

Intending such a powerful opportunity to connect and contribute to your life, as well as, the lives of others, engenders the space for discovering how to become more "at one" with the self you envision. I promise you, making a deliberate attempt to carry out this mission will move you toward establishing your purpose. Ambition to fulfill this purpose will then supply you with the motivation and passion to consummate your divine destiny. Still, in spite of the many quandaries, emotional injuries or frustrations you've encountered, your heart must be open, clear and centered. Otherwise, it will be easy to get preoccupied by people, thoughts and circumstances that are not in alignment with your goals or overall life purpose. Falling into this trap would negate the whole purpose of reading this book, now wouldn't it?

Most of us have a proclivity to make the simple much more complex than it needs to be. Finding your purpose in life is really as unproblematic as discovering what brings you joy and learning how to share it with others who cross your path on a daily basis.

"That's it?" you may be asking. Yes, it is!!!

Here's an analogy to better describe what I attempting to explain: This morning I was awakened with an intention to conduct online research about an idea I had for a future project. As I sat down at my desk with a steamy Chai Tea latte, I noticed that my computer had shut down. There was no power...no blinking green light...no whirs of a cooling fan...just utter silence. Finding this to be odd, considering it was on prior to my going to bed the previous night, I immediately began taking what I thought were the necessary steps to get my office back up and running. I made several phone calls to my service provider, the electrician, the Geek Squad, my landlord...reaching out to anybody and everything I thought could help me get the problem resolved in a timely manner.

After an hour of persuasion, I managed to find myself connecting with technical support via telephone. He was my last hope. I prayed he was competent enough to pull me out of an abyss of mystery that was beginning to consume me with agitation. I'd sipped the last of my tea when the bewildered attendant finally asked me, "Is your computer plugged in?" I am ashamed to say that I was initially annoyed by the simplicity in the resolution he offered. But, something told me to consider his inquiry before I reacted to such absurdity. I, of course, glanced beneath my desk only to discover the computer had been unplugged all along. "OOOOOOHHH, gosh," I exclaimed, "I must have accidentally kicked the cord loose." Instinctively, I reached down and thrust the plug back into the socket. Immediately, all the lights flashed on my computer and I was back in business.

Though I was relieved to have my computer up and running, I couldn't help but think to myself, "I wasted an hour of my time, when all I had to do was look! All I had to do was put the plug into the wall." During my momentary lapse in functionality, I had an epiphany:

Oftentimes, people are not consciously "plugged in" while living their daily lives. This is the overall reason behind why people lose their focus so easily; why their level of cognizance, competence and awareness appears so limited. We try so hard to live in the beginning or the end result of what we aspire to experience, rather than connecting and creating in the space between the source (mind, intelligence, idea, vision, concept, inspiration, etc.) and the created (outcome, product, completed project, acquired job position, etc.). We continuously miss opportunity after opportunity for growth and increase in our relationships, careers, aspirations and wellness by thinking all we need is hope.

We seem to think that aspiration to attain our wildest dreams is all we need to reach our full potential. There is partial truth in this philosophy, but it takes more than just a bit of hope and an idea. There needs to be a vision, an intention and a sense of knowing that radiates from your core. Accomplishment and achievement can't be attained when you are not authentically connected to the "space in-between" that will get you from point A to point B; the space where effort, ambition, energy and focus are exercised. Much like electricity, the current that feeds and fuels – this includes talent, wisdom, insight, ambition and drive – our inner source must be turned on in order to move past "go"; to move from passion into purpose and on to fulfillment.

As obvious as this may sound to some, you would be amazed at how many people are trying to live life in a state of disconnection, wondering why they cannot find their true calling and why their experience of success is limited or skewed. When truth be told, there are an endless amount of possibilities that you can discover and/or endeavor just by being "plugged in" to the space between you and your aspirations.

The ordinary person forgets that our "soul" mission while here on this planet is to ENGAGE IN LIFE; it is the only possible way to properly align yourself with the truest path meant for you to follow in order to get from vision to reality. The key to unleash this concept comes with knowing that the only way you can possibly engage, is to live with passion and the only way to live with passion is to do what you love most.

Once again: the only way you can truly engage in life is to live it with passion and the only way to live with passion is to do what you love most.

Clients, friends and family frequently come to me in search of advice or instruction on how to endeavor the path leading to greatness. Of course, answers to this query are always relevant to each circumstance, as varied advantages or disadvantages surrounding each individual need to be considered. Still, across the board, there are some standard principles that should be considered before one can become invigorated enough to leap over the hurdle of conditioned thinking and into the realization of their dream.

For starters, you must be fanatical about your life vision or mission. If you don't have one…maybe it is time to create one. Your vision should include everything you desire and intend to create, manifest, participate in, or contribute towards through the Higher Self that embodies your unique potential, gifts or talents. Your mission should encompass an overall purpose behind your choice to bring your vision into fruition; an objective that extends beyond your small self, your ego.

Secondly, you must be open to the concept of "waking up" and eradicating the negative thought patterns that have been holding you back or keeping you stagnant.

How do I do this?

Great question.

Keep inquiring until the answer finds you. Trust me, it's there and ready to be heeded the moment you make yourself available to it.

One thing I can assure you, however, is that the answers you seek are not going to appear from the gulf of knowledge you have already grasped. It doesn't matter how educated, well-informed or wise you think you are. There is an adage that says, "your very best thinking got you to exactly where you are today." Quite frankly, your current level of discerning and processing cannot get you to your next level of triumph, love, success or whatever it is you are pursuing, irrespective of how well you've done or how intelligent you think you've become. To improve in any area of your life, you must improve your thinking. In order to grow, you must be willing to expand and increase your mental intake. How far can you really go "if you always do what you've always done; think how you've always thought, or believe the way you've always believed."

Everything you are is culmination or an embodiment of all that you have learned and experienced up until now. It is futile to imagine the possibility of ever rising beyond this point in your life, of ever moving into your fullest potential based on what you already know. If you long to experience increase, success and fulfillment in your life, you must invest time and effort into cultivating new concepts, ideas, and philosophies; absorbing and digesting new beliefs; and trusting yourself to mature within every moment of uncertainty you experience. This can only happen through your willingness to traverse uncharted pathways. Remember: no stream can flow higher than its source. Oftentimes, you may find that the solutions you require come the moment you take one step outside the box of familiarity.

Have you ever stumbled sleepily into the bathroom to take your morning shower, with eager anticipation of feeling a warm, soothing sprinkle of water cascading down your head and back only to be awakened by what feels like millions of freezing pins and needles gushing over your entire body? Initially, it may not have felt so great, but can you remember how alive, charged and revitalized you felt once you stepped outside of the shower and the shock subsided. Much like cold showers, there are certain points in our lives where the responsibility of making major choices and decisions, as well as maintaining commitments while doing our best to sustain balance, can feel completely overwhelming. It is during these types of moments where learning to apply the same process of awakening and rejuvenating our day-to-day can serve to be beneficial to our overall experience in life.

DO SOMETHING

FIND SOMETHING…

…something that can awaken the spirit, shake you out of monotony. Do whatever it takes to get your juices flowing!

A colleague of mine, Danielle Bennett, found herself in a rut a few years ago. She'd just ended a horribly dysfunctional relationship, was recently passed up for a promotion in a dead-end job, lost a dear family member to tragedy, and found herself discontent and living alone in a stuffy, one-room studio apartment. All of this took place in a matter of a year. From the stories she shared, forlorn was the word to best describe her monotonous life – a life she considered doomed and headed straight down a road called, No Where.

At 33, Danielle had reached a point where reflecting over the choices she'd made over the previous ten years had become imperative, especially if she had any intentions on transcending her temporary bout with misery. Through this process she was able to recognize how she'd been "surviving" in a humdrum world for the better part of her adult existence. To top it off, living in the heart of Los Angeles, California, made close to impossible for a single woman without a degree under her belt. Out of all of Danielle's friends, only one of them had a life story dissimilar to her own that amounted to affluence, advanced education or any semblance of ascendency. This, of course, meant that most of the people with whom Danielle associated were pretty much living the same lackluster lifestyle, with very little wherewithal to do anything to bring about change.

So...as far as Danielle could see, her external environment was seemingly appearing as though her chances of ever attaining the dream of being a published author were very slim. Even more overwhelming was the thought of continuing her schooling while working overtime just to catch up on a mountain of overdue bills. From the point of view established through the knowledge and experiences she'd attained up until that point, achievement seemed completely impractical and unfathomable. Still, she refused to let go of the possibility of overcoming these obstacles. The recognition of the value of her talents and a willingness to use them to be of service to others coerced Danielle to start her own freelance writing business. However, living in such an expensive town, she would need to consider alternative options if she were going to get a degree, hold down a decent job, pay a mortgage and run a brand new business – all of which were major milestones in her five year plan.

Though her "current" had been weak prior to this moment of reckoning, Danielle had made great effort to stay "plugged in" to her dream, while never letting go of her "point B". Desperately clinging to what little hope remained inside her heart, she soon surrendered to the notion that "something had to give". Intuition reminded her that something needed to be done; otherwise, she'd find herself spiraling down a path of disappointment and regret.

Vehemently moved to take the necessary plunge into ambiguity – where all things are possible depending upon perception – Danielle was soon standing in front of her boss with a resignation in one hand and her five year plan in the other. This was the one step that essentially added the much-needed shock value to her life that would send her hurdling hungrily into a purpose driven life.

Next step: scrape together her remaining pennies and move clear across country to Atlanta, Georgia – a place where all but one person in the entire state would be complete strangers.

The leap of faith was quitting her job. But, it was in her movement from faith and into the knowing/experiencing side of her dream that inspired her to pack up her car and travel across unfamiliar territories.

Today, six years later, I am proud to say that Danielle's writing business is a success; she has just purchased her first home; and is pursuing a degree in English and Creative Writing. She says, "I had no idea how I was going to get to this point in my life. I just knew I had to move – literally and figuratively. I felt compelled to rise out of monotony and surround myself with new things, faces, situations and environments. Since I didn't know anyone, I had no choice, but to fend for myself...to light my own fire. In each and every little success I made during those first three years, I gained new strengths and capabilities; I continued to grow more empowered to accomplish the next goal and the next and the next... I have much more to do, but I am so glad I moved. It was the best thing I ever did."

How exciting!

Hopefully, Danielle's story gives you a better idea on what I mean when I say, "Be Radical!" There is no feasible way she – or anyone in a position where their backs are against the wall – could have succeeded in this endeavor without first acknowledging the true value of self or the wonder of her gifts and talents. You must be empowered, courageous and confident enough to say to yourself and know that "whatever happens, I WILL NOT give up!" You must also recognize that there is something within you that is meant to be shared – even if it's only with one other person. There is an experience that you know you are meant to have, yet have been incapable of plugging into the source that will ultimately provide you with the energy and power to go after your desired intentions.

It's okay. Today is your day!

Shift your perception. Turn inward to discover your true potential. And once you have done that, begin the path to transcendence and transition by first identifying how to clear out previous conditioning that no longer serves you.

Now that you are aware of the shift that must occur in your thought process, it's now time to consider which actions you must take to carry you through the doors of success or fulfillment. Remember, every success you have, no matter how big or small, IS success. As you move forward, it would behoove you to turn your attention from the things occurring or not occurring, within your external existence. Try your best to start tuning out the distortion – doubts, fears, pains, complaints, competition, judgments, comparisons, etc. – of the world. Swivel your focus inward, onto the beautiful being dwelling inside of you. Let your passion and soul speak to you. Let the murky waters of your mind be purified of confusion as you become one with your authentic self. Replenish it with new thoughts that are more in alignment with the envisioned woman you have made the choice to embrace.

Acknowledge your brilliance, your talent, your value and everything that makes you capable of attaining achievement in every aspect of your life. If your mind is too cluttered to hold all of your ideas, write them down and post them where they are visible to you on a consistent basis. Validate yourself continuously. Waiting for people who could care less about whether or not you achieve your goals to confirm what you already know is no longer an option to consider. Concede to the truth that is you; this includes the good, the bad, the ugly and the pretty; including the razor sharp, but well-intentioned opinions spoken of you by your most loyal, closest friends; even if what they describe looks or sounds nothing like the perception you maintain of self.

Take it all in and care away with what is not accurate about the TRUTH that you are.

As you begin to outwardly manifest the woman within, remember that you are smart. You are powerful. You are divine. You are love. You are intelligent and fully enlightened. You are equipped with all the essential elements you need to make your journey towards success triumphant.

All you have to do now is move!!!! And...as you walk in totality, receptive to the abundance that you've inherited, I invite you to say the following:

I embrace myself as myself, all the while perceiving myself as nothing other than beautiful, gifted, powerful, wise, loving, divinely supported, successful and able. I stand firm in the affirmation that confirms the healing, increased focus, creativity and strength that are essential to carrying out my assignment – my life purpose. I no longer resist or avoid the unique call upon my life which is constantly being revealed to me, as long as I remain open, remembering and recognizing it. I love myself – and my journey – unconditionally. I radiate a fervent passion for what is currently unfolding; for offering my gifts and talents to others in this world; and for simply being true, with ease. Others who cross my path are inspired to do the same as I purposely allow myself to be a living demonstration of possibility. In this now moment, I know the course of my life is no longer the same as the previous, consequent to an enhanced perception of my truest self that I consciously choose to maintain and uphold, without hesitation. Limited conceptions of opportunity are no longer permitted in my mind. On this day, I remember that all that is good about the Creator is good about me.

It is so…and so it is.

Ashe' Amen

"I can only go as far as I AM in my mind! The practice of "being" true and increasing self-awareness neutralizes fear. Fear extinguishes possibility and prevents me from surrendering to passion and destiny."

-        Kimberly E, Banks

Let Go of your But!

From Fear to Freedom

I am optimistic in my beliefs that you are now inspired to unearth the willpower and longing for self-actualization nestled deep inside your heart. I am even more confident that you are also charged with the urge to aim for your desired intentions, goals or life purpose. For this, I must say, you should be very proud. Re-cognize and re-member the honor of having creative aptitude to bring forth something new, something great that can only be borne of you, through you and as you. You are at the point in your life where you are ready to become the personification of the self you envision.

Stay encouraged. Stay focused. Stay open and available. Stay creative.

Whatever, whenever, and however you choose to step forward into your greatness, I gently suggest you to keep one thing in mind: Going against the common grain of mediocrity can be complicated. Being inspired by the text on these pages is one thing; turning inspiration into action is a completely different chore all together. No one said the road to success is an easy one, but there is beautiful and gratifying restitution for those who choose to traverse it. To live past your feelings and move forward with faith is extremely challenging. Trusting yourself to stay in the position of alignment with what you aspire for your life is one of the hardest things you will ever have to do. Maintaining exhilaration, fervency and determination in a society seething with distractions, confusion and destruction is something you are going to have to re-learn. You knew how to do this as a child; at least until you were taught differently. Provision won't always be evident, yet staying, standing and stepping into what is true for you with a level of assurance that all is well, and all is good, is imperative in the pursuit of conquest and achievement.

Along with trying to figure out how to get from point A to point B comes an onslaught of thoughts perpetuated by fear or the lack of confidence in your ability to accomplish whatever it is you endeavor to achieve.

Suppose you want to go back to school and get a degree, lose weight, launch your own business, change careers, start a family or publish your first novel. Exactly what you wish to accomplish is of no relevance to the insight I am sharing with you. We have already climbed that hurdle. What is important, however, is preparation. Now that you are on this quest for expansion and realization, you must prime yourself for the overwhelming sense of uncertainty that comes when one commits to pursuing their goal or their dream. Bear in mind this also pertains to your evolution from the person you no longer wish to be to the person you aspire to become. As you make the first step towards fulfillment, I can guarantee you that unless you are outfitted for the ascent from monotony, the fear of the unknown can get the best of you.

Don't panic. This is merely a feat that must be overcome in order to make it to the next level of self-realization. You now have an opportunity to see fear as a tool for correction or a change in your path that is more in alignment with what you envision. You have the power to perceive the emotion of fear as a "street sign" that is meant to point you in the direction of what you love and a deliberate intention to do everything you can to create it. When properly observed, fear can be useful in your course toward bringing your desires from the imagined to the physical realm. Fear is what increases your awareness of what is possible when you remain conscious of your truth. Belief in ego, the false part of you that entertains the concept of failure, will keep you from a loving awareness that is essential for fruition. Belief in self, where possibility and potential are born, will propel you closer and closer to truth; the root of enlightenment and experiences that exist beyond appearance and circumstance.

"What is the nature of the mind stuff that keeps us in our egos. Ego attachments may be habits of thought, the residue of experiences, desires we've developed and reinforced or have been implanted, even unconscious urges and tendencies. Attachments conspire to create this stuck together bundle of changing thought forms or feelings we label a self...our ego. This sanguine idea of self is just that...an idea – a description of how we are doing in the moment; self-inflated or disappointed. A conglomeration of thoughts, feelings and concepts that changes all the time."

The first step to moving past fear is an acquaintanceship with your true self, an observer of thoughts rather than the follower of ideas and concepts that are dissimilar to goodness, health, wealth, love and peace. The practice of "being" true (as ego-less as possible) and increasing self-awareness neutralizes fear. Fear extinguishes possibility and prevents you from surrendering to passion and destiny.

Over the course of my studies and journey across the country, I have learned that there are really only two emotions that motivate most people throughout their lives. If it isn't clear to you already, those emotions are fear and love. Most of our behaviors and reactions are derivatives of these rooted emotions that sit on two opposing extremes of our responsive compass. What I am saying is that everything you do, think, say and feel is based on whether you love or fear something. This concept also pertains to how you treat people, how passionate you are about something or even finding the courage to move past hindrances.

I will let you in on another little secret! For the sake of disclosure, I am going to first assume that by now you are fully cognizant of a burning urge within you that has been persuading you to do whatever you can to achieve greatness; or at the very least, keeps you clinging "for dear life" to the image of completion interwoven in the fibers of you mind. Yes, I am talking about that thing, that feeling which prompted you to pick up this book in the first place. Well, that fervent and intense need you have to become or create something memorable or remarkable is the very thing I've mentioned on numerous occasions called passion. It is the energy that keeps you moving towards your aspirations, your goals and your dreams; it is what will support you in your intention to turn your dreams into a reality.

So…can we agree now that passion resides on the side of love?

Yes…Great!

Now, if you happen to find yourself lingering on the contrasting side of passion, you are most likely experiencing some form of anxiety or apprehension, wondering if and when you will ever bring the future you envision into your current reality. Why? Good question. Resolution can only come from within; however, it's quite possible that your focus lies more on the possibility of failure and rejection instead of the step-by-step process that will inevitably lead you to into your purpose. Depending on your perception, failure and rejection can be undoubtedly painful. No one likes to endure the unpleasant sentiments that are stirred by disappointment.

With this understanding, from which root emotion do you think thoughts provoked by apprehension and resistance, or cause you to avoid the possibility of failure stem?

If your answer is fear, you are correct.

Fear really comes from a place of darkness where all things negative are born. So, it is easy to see how and why fear prevents most people from tackling their greatest challenges. Reason being is the focus remains on the feelings about what has already happened in the past – to you or someone else you may know. One of the biggest fears that we as women do our best to evade is the miscarriage of our dreams. Who likes to blunder? Why would anyone ever want to fall short of their objectives when the repercussions are so heavy? Living in a space where you can openly embrace disdain from peers and loved ones, or freeing yourself from the burden of self-inflicted guilt, regret and frustration isn't easy. Pondering everything you could have been had you not given up can often keep you diving deeper into an gorge of misery and shame. Such thoughts and judgments don't arouse good feelings, do they?

Suppose I granted you an enchanted power to wipe away all the pain caused by past incidents from your life equation. If I asked you to remove the emotion derived from failed experiences and simply observed them as exactly what they are – experiences, do you think you could do it? Could you possibly change your perception about unpleasant outcomes or unsuccessful attempts in order to start living a purpose driven life? How do you think you would feel if the concept of underachievement was removed from your mind all together? What if you simply chose to view said circumstances as events that merely did not come into existence as you preferred? Could you possibly focus on what has transpired? I believe it would help you to see that the only way you really failed was by giving up or allowing ill-favored results (your own or someone else's) keep you from trying again. The question is…can you believe it.

Here is what I offer for the sake of illumination and understanding: When you expect to experience pain, you experience things painfully. It is when we infuse our love, passion or extreme desire for self-realization into whatever endeavor we intend to pursue that we are able to move past our fears. Successful people are successful because somewhere along the line they have chosen to focus only on their passion and what brings them a sense of fulfillment and joy. Not that they don't feel pain, they simply do not allow agony to remain at the forefront of their mind. Better yet, while the pain may be fully present in their heart and mind, successful people have figured out how to avoid suffering from the dis-ease caused by grief. Thus, they choose to follow the current that propels them into their purpose instead. They choose NOT to focus on the "what ifs", or the "coulda, woulda, shoulda's" when creating the self they desire to manifest. Instead, they concentrate on the "I can", the "I am" and the reality of "what is" in the moment.

The pursuit of accomplishment arouses fear in women because most of us are oblivious as to who really we are or neglect to figure out what our true purpose here on Earth may be. Wait! Before you huff and puff and profess that I don't know what I am talking about, let me clarify. You know you are Miss So and So from Such and Such and that you came from Mr. and Mrs. So and So, whom you identify as your parents. That isn't what I am referring to. When posing the question, "Do you know who you are and what your purpose really is?" seven out of ten women may respond with "I don't know".

But don't fret. There is no judgment here for I have been where you are. I'd like to empower you to dig deeper to find the answer to this question. Don't be forceful in seeking remedy. Allow the response to your query come naturally. If it takes you a couple of days, weeks, or month that is perfectly fine. Let it be so. The objective is to get you to find the answer within you, rather than without. It is there, that is for certain. It just needs to be revealed. Believe me, as daunting as this may sound to you, you won't regret doing the work. It's all a part of the process. Be gentle and patient with yourself.

I will say this again: Follow your passion and you can easily discover whom you are and what you are meant to do in this lifetime.

Do yourself a favor and take a moment to think about who you will be by the time your physical life reaches its end. Compare what you think people will say (be completely honest) about you if your life were come to a close today, verses what you desire for people to say should that day of transition come sooner than you anticipated. Once you have deliberated these inquiries thoroughly, you can choose to mindfully use your answers to align the "you" of today with the perspective path you need to pave in order to merge with the self you see in your heart and mind – the "you" of tomorrow…the you that is true. If you are completely honest with self, the whispers echoing from deep within should include everything from your natural essence to your characteristics to your achievements to your relationships… As you center yourself within the contours of your being, incline your ear to hear the culmination of the services you offered to others and how much of an impact you had on those with whom you shared time and space, however brief.

By doing this, you can get a better gauge on the distance between your current state of being/existing and the self you envision being at the end of your days. This will help you to get a clear indication as to how much work needs to be done between now and then. I am here to tell you, even though it may not seem like it, the person whom you envision in your mind is the person you really are – despite appearance and circumstance. Your objective is to believe she already exists and to be diligent in your journey towards her. Your role in this journey is to be/become the physical personification of that which you envision. Through this experience, you are to know your truth through the constant endeavor to create your way into an authentic state of being that is good, loving, abundant, resourceful, joyous and peaceful.

The notion that bringing to fruition the self you envision is arduous and/or grueling isn't entirely true. It is only true if you make it so by remaining resistant to becoming all you are meant to be. What makes transformation and transcendence in one's life taxing is actually the change that comes as a result of movement out of stagnation, familiarity and comfort. For most, this is an undertaking that feels extremely unpleasant. What we fail to recognize is that disquietude – often perceived as mental, spiritual, emotional, spiritual inconvenience - manifests always for very good reason: to help us know that there is an opposite possibility available for us to create through right mind, right intention and right direction. Conflict or affliction simply lets us know we are off course, out of alignment or headed down a pathway completely irrelevant to the experience of reaching our highest potential or being creative agent for change in the world.

I invite you to remain cognizant of the meaning behind the following statement coined by Dr. Wayne Dyer: Change your mind, change your life. I can assure that if you start focusing your energy on changes essential to your evolution and progress several times throughout your day, instead of the things that appear absent or repulsive, the nasty fears, doubts and disappointments that have kept you from attaining your hopes and dreams will dissolve. You see, we are frequently tempted to define ourselves through the past experiences we've endeavored. We mainly model and mold ourselves from the culmination of pessimistic views, judgments and reservations harbored in our hearts and minds, despite the fact that they impede growth, improvement and increase. This is so easy to do because we've been conditioned to do so from the day we were born. And now, being that doing the work to remove unhealthy thoughts and infirmities is toilsome, we find ourselves taking a less demanding route by focusing our attention to what we do not have, as well as what we have yet to accomplish.

Why not...it is easier...right?

When things do not work out as we envisioned, we allow our emotions to take over our consciousness. Our ego coerces us to entertain a myriad of negative beliefs and opinions, all of which are designed to keep us feeling insignificant, powerless, unworthy, or incapable. The continuous reiteration of ineffectiveness is outpoured into our life, therefore justifying mediocrity or inferiority. It provides the space between which we can place blame for our shortcomings. Neglecting to reach our goals ultimately adds to the adverse perception we have of ourselves and preserves the already distrustful concept we hold about life. In an attempt to reach blindly for anything to make us "right" about who we think we are in this world, we constantly run into reminders made evident through what we haven't completed or been able to accomplish.

...And the never-ending cycle continues.

Why...because what we focus on most is exhibited in our external environments, circumstances and relationships. Perpetuating thoughts of lack, insecurity, fear and doubt can only create more of what you don't want in your life. This insight is better explained in the beautiful awareness penned by the phenomenal spiritual writer, Paul Ferrini, in his book titled Love Without Condition: "The cynical nature of thought and action bring up continual lessons for you. The lessons always underscore the gap between what you want and expect will happen and what appears to manifest in your life....this dilemma is necessary for your learning...It is inevitable that you will focus your attention on people and things outside of you. This is the world of "conditions." It cannot give you what you want. It can only reflect back to you what you don't want."

In order to create/experience more of what you want in your life, it is wise to 1) focus on what is going on inside of you, rather than outside of you, 2) see the lessons, rather than the discomfort of disenchantment, 3) be mindful of your thoughts and actions, 4) align yourself with people who exemplify your deepest hopes and aspirations, and 5) practice saying "yes" to possibilities that seem beyond your grasp; "yes" to the understanding that you are being called forth to do a unique thing on this planet; "yes" to the announcement of your radical unfolding that is to be expressed as your individual – but never separate – life. This means focusing on all that is good and feels "right" for you. It entails recognizing that you are worthy of healing, evolution, progress, increase, change, release and the physical expression of that which dwells inside your imagination. It involves remaining present to the mindset of living and not just surviving through the gap between life and death.

Embracing the awareness above is how paradigm shifts essential for you to thrive and flourish beyond that which you already know unfold. This is how you are able to courageously relinquish smallness and dive spontaneously into bigness. This is how you are able to extract the gifts of divinity from within. This is how you will be able to offer the world the same inspiration through which you are able to epitomize love, wisdom, intelligence, brilliance and oneness. This is how you will be able to honor, respect and connect with not only everyone that exists in this world, but also the Most High Source from which you flow. This is how you will be able to tap into your own well of power, intelligence, wisdom and creativity and give birth to possibility. This how you will be able to answer the call for your life.

Understand what's been imparted to you above and you will undoubtedly supersede mediocrity and ascend into you inherent space of excellence. Trust this with all your heart. For to the degree of your belief is your ability to transcend, transition and transform your circumstances.

If you think long and hard enough, you can discern how easily you allow debilitating thoughts to remain in the center of your attention. Now, maybe you have an idea as to why you have remained in that same place for such a long time.

Now, let's get back to the concept of freeing yourself from fear.

Let me share a few words with you that I picked up from renowned, best-selling spiritual author, Neale Donald Walsch. He wrote, "In the moment you pledge your highest love, you greet your greatest fear." Fear, among other things, is the most common reason why we as women have a hard time letting go of our "buts" – literally and figuratively. Eliminating, confronting or working through your fears is a must if you intend to achieve anything in life; if you intend to become something other than what you already are; if you intend to move past where you are; if you intend to become that which you truly were born to be. In fact, if you aren't afraid about achieving a particular aspiration, you are wasting your time fiddling with things, situations, people and places that restrict contribution to the enhancement of your overall greatness. Other than procrastination (a topic we will explore in a later chapter), there is no viable reason why it has taken you so long to execute a venture, plan, aspiration or desire that gives you no pangs about achieving it.

What are you waiting for?!!! Things to be easy? ...and then what?

If it's menial, GO AHEAD and get it over with. Mark the task off your "To Do" list and move on to an endeavor that may be a little more challenging, or provokes some sense of anxiety that is worth your effort to conquer.

Some would argue that the greater the fear, the bigger the dream. Depending on your outlook, you may also agree. For the sake of deliberation, I encourage you try to entertain a different thought, even if just for a moment. Imagine that instead of being consumed by fear and letting it deter you from a specific outcome you envision in your mind, you have found a way to utilize the energy behind your trepidation to help you strive harder; to somehow turn negative energy into positive; to bring what you once considered impossible to the realm of possibility.

Now here is the key that unlocks the truth about your fear of failing or falling short of your potential and ability: whenever dread arises, try NOT to visualize your overall goal in its entirety. Attempt to look at it in bits and pieces that can be properly and strategically placed into position with the aim of making your whole dream complete. Another way to look at it is through the eyes of Martin Luther King, Jr., who once said, "You don't have to see the whole stair case, just take the first step." Change your perception; alter how you see your goal. As long as you do this, you will discover that the large, overwhelming goal is constantly presenting you opportunities to create many smaller goals that are much easier to attain. I assure you, you will be greatly rewarded by this deed alone, as things will begin to look a lot less frightening.

In knowing that our steps toward the unfolding of our lives have already been ordered, we can experience ease and grace by changing our perspective, our position. Through the words of inspirational, Hollywood "superhero," Will Smith, we are reminded to scale down our strides in the journey to self-actualization. He says, "We make life more complex, when it is really simple. You don't set out to build a wall. You don't start with the vision of building that biggest, baddest wall in the history of mankind. You start by saying 'I am going to take this one brick and lay it as perfectly as a brick can be laid.' You do that every single day and soon you have a wall."

To overcome the things that impede furtherance and fruition, you can first begin with recognizing and allowing yourself to confront what it is that brings you fear - False Evidence Appearing Real. And secondly, try your best to get to the root cause of such fears and inhibitions, which most likely were developed in the earlier years of your childhood. Ask yourself, "When was the first time I experience this fear? What was I doing, and what occurred that made me feel unsafe about being who I truly am?"

This is a powerful question that can bring about a greater awareness that will help you overcome your greatest challenges, and put your biggest buts behind you for good.

Now you have the secret!

Understanding that fear is false evidence appearing real brings forth an awareness that everything that you thought could keep you from your goals no longer exist. In fact, it never really did. Everything you consider fearful can only appear as such to the degree and ability in which you are able to perceive them to be.

Besides the fear of rejection and failure that I mentioned earlier, let's look at some other things that make people cower to the preemptive punches that successful people circumvent. Lack of money, time or resources are definitely some illusions that keep some people from even taking that first step to achievement and prominence. Limited education, information and technical skills are some other things that prevent people from building momentum. Age is another major issue of concern when it pertains to the pursuit of fulfillment.

I cannot stress this next point enough: You are NEVER too old and it is NEVER too late to realize your most esteemed aspirations, especially in this day and age where technology and the availability of resources are at our fingertips.

Truth be told, fathoming the reality of actually living a dream is often times the very thing that discourages people from success and/or fulfillment. From time to time, the image we hold of ourselves in an instance where our vision actually reaches fruition can be quite overwhelming. Excitement and elation, consequent to thoughts of gratification enters our hearts and mind, can be easily obliterated by the disappointment we feel when we ponder potential failure. It is often the big picture that causes people to become enveloped by inertia. What I usually advise clients when this happens is to write out on a piece of paper a description of their "big picture". Once completed, I then encourage them to dissect that big picture into smaller pictures – ones that seem much easier to attain; especially as it pertains to getting from point A to point B. Through this action, my clients are then able to at least break free of the preverbal bars that hold them prisoners inside their own minds.

While we are at it, I think now would be a great time to look at the context behind the word freedom. Just briefly, I want you to contemplate the meaning of this word really carefully so that it may be applied to your life and the way you choose to live it from this point forward. Now, by society's definition, the word freedom entails a state in which a person is able to act and live as he or she pleases without being subject to undue restraints or restrictions. Or as it relates to captivity, freedom can be described as being released or rescued from physical binding, enslavement, and confinement, or imprisonment. In the previous chapter, I spoke of how much time my friend Danielle spent dwelling inside her own form of mental prison throughout the better part of her adult life. Why? It's simple. She wasn't yet gifted with the awareness of knowing that doing nothing about her state of existence was what kept her stagnant and immobile. The moment she moved is the moment her life changed. Nine times out of ten, if we are not leading successful lives it is because we are being held captive by our own fears. Now, for the sake of freeing yourself from apprehension, I will reiterate the objective of this chapter once more. Make your greatest effort to rescue yourself from the mental and emotional barricades that keep you from succeeding by placing one foot in front of the other. Do something!!!!! Try something!!! If you fail...do not allow fear to grow. Try something else!!! Do anything that gets you out of captivity.

What if I told you that as long as you attempt to achieve, you could NEVER really fail? You may fall short a time or two, but you can never truly fail. My mother always told me as a young child: nothing beats a failure but a try. Great words of wisdom, wouldn't you say? SO you see...this means that if you don't meet your desired deadline or outcome, your goal is still ahead of you. AGAIN, the only person who can really keep you from reaching a goal is you. True, things come up, obstacles may fall along your path, but it is YOUR choice to stay stuck; your choice to turn around and go back; or your choice to uncover the courage within you and find any means necessary to get around the impediment standing before you.

Lovingly coerce yourself to do what you are afraid to do. Confront your fears and they have no choice but to disappear. Push through your obstacles. Renounce your need to know any specific results (how or when) in your pursuit. This is not to say to let go of the intended outcome or the forecasting vision of your endeavors, but rather LET GO of the need to reach that particular result or the feelings behind it. Recognize that there is "more than one way to skin a cat." Limiting yourself to one means of manifestation decreases your chances of creating opportunities and welcoming possibilities of fruition, simply because you are unable to recognize them consequent to being steadfast and resolute. There is a big difference in focusing on what it is you

103

would like to accomplish and needing to fulfill it for the sake of reward or recognition, or for the sake of satisfying your ego through the attainment of validation from your peers. It is exactly the need and the expectation of how, when and what will happen, or how you will feel when you finally make it across the finish line, that can distract you from your objective. As long as you stay emotionally attached to your goals, you will be forever attached to the fear of NOT achieving them. Simply focus on your plan of action, sharpen your skills and immerse yourself into the passion of doing what you love and cherishing the journey. If you do this, there is no way you can fail. It is impossible to fall short of becoming your intended self if you simply follow your bliss; pursue what you love; enjoy work that makes you happy.

In the awe-inspiring movie about faith, *The Peaceful Warrior*, an unorthodox teacher confronts a resistant student – a gymnast – about letting go of his ego in order to overcome the obstacle of acquiring a career-ending injury in hopes of competing again. Instead of focusing on the possibilities of success, the student remained consumed in the notion of blaming those he felt were responsible for his misfortune, including himself. Not to mention, his desire to rise above circumstances was lost in his inability to relinquish his anxiety of being injured again. In the student's refusal to accept accountability, the wise teacher felt compelled to convey a lesson that ultimately presented a shift the student's thinking.

"I have a gift for you, but you have to come with me in order to get it," the teacher offers. "I want you to meet me at the park in the foothills tomorrow morning and we will go."

Wallowing in pity, the only thing the student heard in the statement was the word "gift". Thus, feeling deserving of something that would bring about a sense of elation, the student shows up the following morning filled with anticipation. Upon arrival, the teacher hands the student a backpack filled with water and snacks. Confused, the student asks, "What is this? I thought you said you had something for me." The teacher replies, "I do, but you have to follow me in order to get it."

Up the mountain the two of them hiked. Two hours into the climb, the student begins to complain, vocalizing his regret for following the teacher on what was beginning to look like a silly journey to nowhere. Nonetheless, the idea of receiving his promised gift urges him forward. Four hours later, so anxious about receiving his reward, the student starts to express his annoyance.

"How much further do we have to go?"

"It's just up the way," the teacher replies calmly.

The two of them continue without another word. An hour later, when the two of them finally reach the mountaintop, the teacher spreads his arms and takes in the panoramic view of the city below. Not quite understanding the reason for the teacher's sudden jubilation, the student begins to inspect the surroundings, searching for clues that would unveil the gift that his teacher promised to give him. Once again irritated by finding nothing but shrubbery, rocks and dirt, yet still excited about the possibility of gaining something new, the student asks, "Where is my gift?"

A few seconds pass before the teacher says, "It's right here. Don't you see it?"

Again the student pans the view. "Am I missing something? I don't see anything up here that could possibly qualify as a gift."

"Aren't you excited? I mean, you were excited the entire way up here, knowing that you were going to get something?"

"Yes, but now that we are here...this is it? You mean to tell me I wasted my whole day climbing a mountain just to look at a bunch of dirt?"

The teacher bends down, picks up a rock and hands it to the student. "Okay then...Here you go."

He smiles wide as he does this, already knowing that it would only be a matter of seconds before student understood his words.

Sure enough, the student begins to grin and playfully tosses the rock back to his teacher. "I get it."

You see, the teacher was trying to show the student that it was the journey to the gift that is often times more exciting than actually arriving to the destination, but it depends on perception and perspective. The entire way, the student never took his thoughts off of getting the gift therefore his journey up the mountain was filled with excitement. It wasn't until he reached the mountaintop that he felt disappointed. And that was only because the outcome he anticipated did not turn out to be what he expected. But I promise you one thing; he will never forget the journey up the mountain. Needless to say, the seed of motivation was planted as soon as he accepted his invitation, not upon his arrival to the top of the mountain. The rest of the movie entails a quest of conquering defeat that eventually enables the student to stake his claim of being the true champion he saw living inside himself.

We cannot speak of overcoming fears and making our way into freedom without touching on the importance of faith, courage and confidence. Gauging the distance between your current self and your desired self is one way to help boost your confidence, which will then awaken the faith and courage you need to transcend limitations – physically or mentally. It also helps to determine whether you are being lazy and need to push a little harder, or if you are right where you need to be. The road to self-actualization is not as hard or off-putting if the path chosen is cherished along the way.

It doesn't happen overnight, however. Being aware of your choices, as well as the outcomes that are created as a result of your choices is another way to gauge how close to fruition you are. As you start to recognize the closing gap between the two selves (present and envisioned), you begin to gain momentum and with that momentum comes confidence. One thing you cannot bypass to get to confidence and courage is faith. You MUST BELIEVE you are capable and that you WILL succeed, no matter how many attempts it takes, in whatever it is you are pursuing. You must hold allegiance to yourself and your purpose without wavering from your beliefs. Stay devoted to and diligent in trusting your abilities or you will NEVER make it from concept through to creation. The smallest amount of doubt makes it impossible.

Remember these words: What you resist, persists. What you conceive, can be achieved. If you continue to cower to your fears, they will never go away. It isn't until you confront them that they will cease to exist and you can make your way towards freedom. Perceiving them is the ONLY way you can begin to figure out how conceive a way to alleviate them. One of the easiest ways to overcome fear is to make the decision to constantly strive towards being the person you envision in your mind. Of course, I encourage you to engage yourself in the workbook activities that accompany this book in order to help you to get a clearer picture of who you are and what you are here to experience. You will be empowered to monitor the choices and decisions you make as they pertain to who and what you are most passionate about.

Seek happiness, alignment and love before all else in your quest to overcome your fears. It is exactly the fuel you will need to remain on course. Joy and elation are emotions that will catapult you past fear and into the presence of affirmation, pride, love and enlightenment. Pace yourself. This is not something you want to rush. Savor the moments of your freedom with each broken barrier.

Enjoy the journey.

"I'd be frightened by not using whatever abilities I'd been given. I'd be more frightened by procrastination and laziness."

-      Denzel Washington

Let Go of your But!

Emancipation Procrastination

As of now you have made several tremendous breakthroughs on your road to success, fulfillment, joy, happiness, etc. You now realize that reaching your greatest potential is based on your desire to utilize your gifts and talents – not just for self, but also as service towards others; you've allowed honesty with self to lead you towards discovering your true value and worth; you've taken a glimpse of your current state of being and matched it with your desired legacy – what people will say about you when you leave this earth; you have even succumbed to the relentless urge to do more with your life and do away with the negative self-talk derived from past experiences. And lastly, you have freed yourself from the fear by which you have been held hostage over the last several years.

Whew…that's quite a bit to digest.

I applaud you for taking such a big step in letting go of your buts and mastering your life.

Now give yourself permission to take a huge breath and EXHALE!!! Release every negative thought that attempts to infiltrate your mind in this moment. Stay in the space of self-love, nurturing and empowering thoughts that perpetuate inspiration and motivation for "right mind" and "right action" towards that which you envision. Practice doing this for the remainder of the day.

I compliment and commend your desire to celebrate. You deserve it. Keep in mind however, that there is still work to be done. Hopefully, the baggage and cloaks of your past that have kept you mentally imprisoned – until today – are slowly beginning to dissipate. Well, at least most of it. And now, there you stand. Completely naked and void of any and all excuses as to why you can't succeed at what you do best. I dare you to stand in front of the mirror and peer deep into the eyes of the person staring back at you. Are you able to do so without catering to harmful thoughts or reasons as to why you are not good enough, not ready, not equipped to leap beyond the limitation of you? Are you able to embrace yourself, praise yourself, tell yourself that the time has come for you to rise, to step into your blessings and miracles that are meant to happen through and for you? Are you even able to tell yourself just how much you love yourself; just how much you are worthy of exactly what you aspire and desire; just how beautiful you are in the eyes of the Creator; just how perfectly able you are RIGHT NOW to LET GO and LET BE?

Trust me. I understand how hard it is to do this. Imagining it is one thing, but actually telling yourself that you are worth everything you desire – love, support, self-realization, appreciation, compassion, empathy, understanding, etc. – is much more difficult than most are willing to admit. It's amazing how we have a tendency to expect others to express these types of things we are unable to express them to ourselves. Something to contemplate is this: contingent upon your level of belief, you are the YES to possibility and the channel through which it comes into fruition; or…to the degree of your disbelief, you are the NO to possibility and the hindrance of manifestation.

Standing exposed, with nothing between you and the imagined self can create the space for the churning of venomous thoughts and negative self, that if not controlled will flutter throughout your mind like aimless butterflies. Among them, "which step do you take first?" ring the loudest.

This is a great place to start, for here is where I will offer that you begin to trust that all the answers you need to persevere, triumph or succeed are already available to you. You need do nothing but ask and get quiet. Even when you don't know what questions to ask in order to get the answers you need, start believing that the heart has a way of sending requests to the Universe in such a way that the mind may not be able to articulate. Your hearts desires alone have the power to attract exactly what you need, at any given moment. Again, it is to the degree of your belief that resolution to your challenges are able to transpire.

It is when we doubt, fear the appearance of lack, or cater to sentiments "not enoughness" that we get caught in the web of dream miscarriages and letdowns. We start to focus on what can't be done or the illusion of impossibility, which eventually gives birth to overwhelm. Here is where a handy dandy, piece-by-piece plan (a dissection of the whole vision into tiny, bearable portions) we spoke about earlier will serve in helping you map out your route to destiny. But wait, you don't have one yet, do you? Well, get on it. There is no time like today.

This is usually where procrastination comes into play.

The intention starts with creating a plan. Notice as you move towards your desk to sit down to map out your plan that will encompass the next one, three or five years of your life, you've already become preoccupied with distractions and thoughts that probably do not coincide with your plan to sit down and plan. For starters, your office is in disarray. The telephone just rang and it is your long lost cousin Bertha who needs a full play-by-play about your life over the last ten years. Your husband is hungry and your daughter can't find her favorite red crayon… This is where you put off your plan for making "the plan" until tomorrow, right? Or the next day…or how about next month…

Is that a choice that is in alignment with what you aspire to create for you?

Considering you have gotten this far in the book, I am not surprised by your motivation. I commend you for setting aside the sense of unworthiness, no longer choosing to be intimidated by the challenges that come with pursuing your ambitions. I applaud your for finding the inspiration to transcend dark, abhorrent reservations and move toward the light of success and self-actualization. My question is: why are you so easily distracted?

The problem here is the resilient undercurrent of resistance that carries with it the answer as to why some people remain unsuccessful. Plenty of which has to do with the fear of failure, but being that we have already nipped that issue in the "but", let's explore some other reasons as to why you may find yourself trapped in a never-ending cycle of procrastination.

If you sound anything like the person I just described above, it is quite possible that you have poor time management. However, if you choose to search deeper into the functionality beneath your pile of distractions, you may possibly find yourself in such an unclear state because you are apprehensive about where to begin? Or, is it possible that you are unwilling to commit to completing the tasks you start, just in case the venture turns out to be much more difficult than you envisioned?

Ask yourself these questions: Does being an underachiever feel much safer than having to justify a failed attempt if you actually pursued your greatest challenge or aspiration? Are you choosing to clutter your mind and environment with a plethora of negative energy and "what ifs" simply because you don't feel worthy of taking the next most appropriate steps towards achievement? Do you feel that you are not ready to be in the limelight and ill-prepared to take on the responsibilities that come with triumph? And lastly, does the idea that "to whom much is given, much will be required" frighten you?

I would hope that your answers to the questions above are "no". If this is not the case, I encourage you to take the time to do a bit of soul searching. Don't be afraid to put the book down for a while, take a walk around the park and commune with your natural self, your heart, your Creator. Use the time to pinpoint exactly what it is that keeps you terrified or feeling undeserving of success? Without harboring too much on the past, try to identify the moment you were made to feel undeserving and incompetent? Most likely this occurred somewhere in your distant past, or even your childhood. It may involve more than a 45 minute walk on the trail to estimate the root cause and/or eradicate conflicting thoughts and conditionings. Here is a suggestion: Taking the time to assess your patterns should be cornerstone of you plan.

Let me back pedal for a second. In the event that you happen to be an avid list maker, I want to bring a very small but prevalent issue in this discussion to your attention. As good as it is to see the steps that will inevitably lead you to your goal; there are some drawbacks that can hinder you if you are not careful in your list making. You see, in the act of creating a humongous "to do" list, you can temporarily distract yourself from the main task at hand. IF you find yourself going down a list of things, checking them off as you complete them, be careful not to become consumed by adding more to the list as it begins to shorten. Stay focused on purpose and what tasks will lead you towards achievement. Refrain from getting caught up in making sure you stay busy in order to avoid stagnation or idle time. It is very easy to simultaneously find yourself further and further way from achievement than you really intended when you sat down and started your list. Without your knowing, your list has now become a key player in the game of procrastination.

On the topic of prevailing over your tendency to dawdle as a result of apprehension, become immersed in a dialogue with the "self" that you envision. Allow yourself to hear her voice and let her share with you the real reasoning behind your procrastination. Ask her: Are you afraid of failing? What do you think will happen to you if you fail? Why are you afraid of commitment? What makes you ill prepared for what success will bring? And lastly, what would you do and how would you go about doing it if you weren't afraid?

After you discover the answers to these questions, gauge whether or not they are worthy of keeping you from a life filled with prosperity, joy, peace, fulfillment and abundance. Are they worth forfeiting an overall sense of accomplishment that comes with being committed to completion? Are your justifications for procrastination really worth despair, discontentment and overwhelming sentiments of letdown that will follow you for years, reminding you every day what you failed to become? If I had to answer for you, I would say MOST CERTAINLY NOT!!

I   am compelled to encourage you to be more than a sloth! You've heard all the clichés that hint to how "tomorrow is never promised". You are probably saying to yourself that acting on the urge to be more than what you are in this moment (which by the way is perfectly fine) isn't as simple as I am proposing. You think that there is much more to be done even before you decide to step into your destiny. Soon you will see, that making the choice to step forward really is…all that simple. No matter if you are physically motionless or mentally inert, the bottom line is that procrastination is a choice.

Let's get technical for a moment. There are five elements that are determining factors on whether or not a person will choose procrastination as a lifestyle: the existence or deficiency of emotional strength, well-directed thought processes, efficient time-management skills, control over habits, and the ability to complete tasks. If you are weak in all of the areas listed above, I can just about bet my savings that you have a hard time overcoming procrastination. Needless to say, in order to overcome what you may feel to be a minor but constant battle with postponing your dreams, enroll in the opportunity to work on developing better control of your emotions, focusing attention and thinking rationally; also learn how to self-manage your time and life, change your bad habits, and acquire better task completion and problem solving skills.

The most common form of procrastination I see today is when people use their bills, mortgage and car note as reason for not leaving their job to pursue their true passion. I see people putting off their dreams for one more week, one more month, or one more year longer than they really should in order to "prepare" for the road ahead. Don't get me wrong; I am also guilty of having done the same in previous years. All for the simple notion of thinking I had to wait until I had the right amount of money in the bank, a new job opportunity presented itself or I felt I'd acquired enough skills and confidence to traverse the path of an entrepreneur. If you are procrastinating, some of these excuses may sound a lot like yours.

I say to you lovingly, STOP IT!!

Do yourself a favor and think about what you are really losing in your efforts to "get prepared" for the right moment, the right time or the right environment and circumstances. I am not insinuating that you quit your job today and dive head first into a pool of uncertainty. Considering that following your passion involves taking risks, you still have to be somewhat logical. What I am implying is this: sometimes planning becomes another device for procrastination. You can plan until you are as blue as a Smurf, yet it can't be truly beneficial to your life until you actually make that sacrificial step outside of your comfort zone. If you are going to plan – which I strongly suggest – YOU MUST prepare yourself to ACT and you must ACT NOW. No need putting off what you could do today...you know the saying.

Trust me; there is ALWAYS something – big or small – that you can do every single day to put you closer to accomplishing your goals. Discover what these things are and do them, one by one. Do not let another day go by without being productive and proactive about eliminating procrastination.

Depending on how you choose to spend it, time can either be your best ally or your worst enemy. There are really only two ways to deal with procrastination. The avoidance of dealing with the matter just won't do. However, getting to the underlying, core issue or cause for your procrastination is the best way to "attack" it. Once you find out what the root cause for your tendency to "put off" certain aspects of your life (because this is essentially what you are doing), you either bust right through it or you cower to its power and continue evading your goals all together. You either strangle the life out of it or it will definitely strangle the life out of you and your intentions. Hasn't time already proven this?

Again, right here, right now, in this very moment is where you make the choice to become a radical participant in your own life. It's up to you and only you to combat this invisible nemesis. As you prepare for the overthrowing of this nasty adversary, put every ounce of your energy, love, passion and heart into it. You can't offer a preemptive punch without having the will to back it up should procrastination choose to fight back. It is the only way your efforts will be effective. The exercise of willpower into your efforts to emancipate yourself from procrastination is crucial. Through this practice you will be better equipped and cognizant of the evidence which proves you can only get out of life exactly what you put into it. If not, all you will have at the end of the day, and the next, and the next, is cluttered mind like that of a woman's closet.

I, like most women, used to have a habit of collecting shoes, garments and accessories and keeping them until the fashion cycle repeated itself; And when it did, I remained forever thankful for the chance to don my "newly used" threads for the second time in one decade.

Times have changed. The reality is – I don't need to keep things in my closet that I don't use. Hoarding the old (the past) doesn't do anything but create clutter and takes up space that could be used to create new experiences (the present). I now take pleasure in purchasing new shoes or garments, and heading straight for my closet to purge any out dated items before infusing the new ones into my wardrobe. If I haven't worn something in two to three years, out the window I toss it. The same standard is applicable to the life I now lead. Thus, I have no room for distractions that may encourage postponement of things or activities that are vital to my success as a business woman. I guarantee you this: you can tell a lot about a woman depending on how well she maintains her closet. It is a direct reflection of what is going on in her mind.

I offer that you use this illustration as inspiration to take self-inventory and clear out the space in your mind and in your life. Weed out all those piles of uncompleted tasks, unfulfilled dreams and unrealistic goals. Exchange them with a collection of measurable intentions and achievable strategies coupled with an arsenal of affirmation and unbreakable desire to see your goals through to the end. Create a new practice that compels you to discard "clutter" as soon as it has been handled, managed or completed. Extinguish any regret, anger, or unforgiveness (even of self) by confronting them in a healthy manner so that you can move forward clearly, without hindrance from the present into your future, rather than teetering statically with one foot in the past and one in the present. Embrace change. Learn to "let go" in transition without giving situations, events, people, and relationships more energy than necessary. Do away with the tendency to let things linger as if they will somehow disappear or work themselves out on their own. Understand that this includes all of your   and pain regarding perceived failures, not just projects, goals and relationship. Stop hoarding what no longer serve you. Trust that if something is not working or has failed worked for some time, the time has come for you to LET IT GO!!! Accept the truth of its position. Erase the "but" that keeps you unnecessarily attached so that you can work with the space and freedom to create from the presence of "what is" rather than from "what isn't."

Successful people ALWAYS CHOOSE NOW. We – that's right, I am talking about you and I – don't wait until later to sort through the mail or pay our bills at the very last minute. The moment something arises is the best time to take care of it, whether it involves checking emails, returning a phone call, setting an appointment or running an important errand. This alone keeps your list of 'to dos" as short and clutter free as possible.

Understand that freeing up your time and emancipating yourself from procrastination is a small debt to pay in comparison to the rewards you will reap when you finally reach your goals. In terms of pay off, another issue that people use to justify procrastination is money – not having enough of it, or not wanting to sacrifice deficiency for the sake of a dream. People do not realize how much their life is governed by money. Truth be told, that without the constant practice of centering my mind and clearing out negative thoughts, I am no exception. Think about it: How often do we go shopping without making an inquiry about how much something costs?

Almost NEVER.

Next time you go shopping, watch your actions as your peruse the aisles, searching for an item that will bring about a sense of delight. Pay close attention to the thoughts that begin to

120

stir while going through your process of choosing. The first thing you do is pick up the desired object for inspection. I'm certain you agree that purchasing something you don't like or doesn't fit your standard of quality is not the wisest choice to make. So…now that you have picked out the object of your desire, what is the next thing that happens? That's right…you look for the tag. Why? Because this will determine whether or not you will place the item into your cart or shove it begrudgingly back on the shelf. Wouldn't it be great to get to the point where you never have to look at the price of something you want to purchase? How amazing it must feel to purchase whatever we want without being deterred by a simple figure on a tiny price tag.

In taking a sidebar, I will say that until one has fully mastered the Law of Attraction, the best bet as it pertains to entertaining lack in life is to make the decision to change your perception about money. In my studies of Metaphysics (meta – meaning beyond; physics – relating to the physical realm from where belief, trust, faith and creativity are centered) over the years, I have learned the very valuable interpretation of money: M.O.N.E.Y - my own natural energy yield, which is the true premise of living in abundance. To be more specific ponder what spiritual guidance examiner, Asandra Lamb, writes about this topic.

"If our "energy yield" is not yielding very much, this becomes an opportunity to heal something that is interfering with our ability to RECEIVE…The first level of understanding has to be that wealth does not come by accretion. It comes because of our ability to accept love and support from Source. Prosperity comes because we have expanded from within, not by trying to accumulate wealth from without."

I offer that you pick up a copy of *The Abundance Book* by John Randolph Price, to get more acquainted with the Law of Abundance. Now, if this is your first time exploring such a concept, understand that this way of "being" (not doing) takes plenty of mental reconditioning and centering your heart. It has to become a daily habit, even if you spend fifteen, twenty or thirty minutes a day of spending time reflecting over your thoughts, choices and decisions. It entails doing away with toxic or insignificant thoughts that are focused on lack and replacing them with more natural thoughts and affirmations centered on receiving goodness. This will eventually shift your attitudes and beliefs about money and the availability of it.

Don't get me wrong. I am keen on the idea that you may be holding a job that pays well. Working the traditional 9 – 5 is wonderful and commendable if it is truly what you desire. If you are working at a job, staying "just over broke" until you "have enough money" to leave, recognize that you are still trading talent and time for money. My point here is that waiting for the right opportunity, the right job, or the right salary is like waiting for someone else to hand you your dream in a warm, cuddly blanket. It doesn't work that way. YOU have to spend whatever it takes to invest in YOUR dream. No one else is obligated to do so. It is YOUR dream. YOU have to create the right opportunity. YOU have to pursue the job you truly desire. And here's to thinking outside the box: YOU may have to CREATE your dream job (start your own business, consult or partner with others to provide a service), which would ultimately mean that YOU won't have to settle for a meager salary of which someone may or may not feel you are worthy. By waiting on these things to be handed to you is another form of dream suicide. It is very much like waiting on someone else to tell you, "Okay, you can have your dream now" or "mmmmmmm…I don't think you are quite ready to reach your goals…better give it a few more years."

How ludicrous? Well…how much do you value yourself, your talents and your time?

Remember the infamous saying from the movie, *Field of Dreams*, "Build it…and they will come." It suggests that you envision your dream, develop a plan, stick to it and open your mind and heart to every possible possibility that can possibly manifest. Surrender to this awareness and you'll notice how all the key elements to reaching fruition will begin to appear. Everything you require or desire is made evident contingent upon your level of belief that it already exists. I guarantee that if you keep yourself available and aware to this process at all times, you'll soon realize that everything you ask for, you will or have already received. Again, need I remind you that you, along with your perceptions about whatever occurs are the only things keeping your from or propelling you towards success and the attainment of your deepest desires.

Don't waste another minute. Each and every excuse you utter – however valid it may be – is only going to keep you further and further from your goals. Even the time and energy it takes to come up with a "justifiable" reason for your procrastination takes up valuable time that could be used in a more productive fashion. So…your best bet is to sit down, put some serious thought into why you continue to put off doing what could be accomplished today. Better yet, put forth the effort to invest more time into figuring out why and how you CAN begin to live the life to which you aspire.

Let Go of your But!

"It's vital that you accept yourself and learn to be happy with who God made you to be. If you want to truly enjoy your life, you must be at peace with yourself...God wants you to have a good life, a life filled with love, joy, peace, and fulfillment. That doesn't mean it will always be easy, but it does mean that it will always be

GOOD!"
-       Joel Osteen

Gracious Gratitude

*I*t is a well-known notion throughout the health industry that the most nourishing of all human emotions is gratitude. Often times we are not aware of just how harmful the act of complaining or resenting circumstances can be to our authentic self, not to mention those around us. We fail to contemplate the impact that harboring negative thoughts can have in our lives. I wrote briefly in previous chapters on how to stamp out past conditionings and change your mind set in order to overcome fear and procrastination. In this chapter I will discuss other key elements that can be useful in the task of letting go of your buts. Most important of them all, however, is the practice of being more aware of the WORDS spoken from your mouth, especially amidst a sudden moment of dissatisfaction.

Are you a grumbler? Do you express discontent for every little situation that bothers you? Do you make effort to solve problems or are you a contributor to every problem that surfaces in your life? Surprisingly, there are people who are clueless about how they show up or contribute to what transpires in their lives. This is because they have no idea that what they may be experiencing has a direct reflection of what's going on within. Therefore, they have a tendency to perceive and experience themselves as victims of the dramatic occurrences that transpire in their world.

I suppose before we go any further, it would be a good idea to determine whether or not this can be attributed to the likes of you.

How can you do this?

I want you to begin observing the words you speak throughout your daily affairs. Be mindful of just how often disdain for people, events and circumstances are spewed from your lips without as much as a second thought. Every single person on this planet is guilt of doing this at some point or another, so no need to feel ashamed. Simply be honest with yourself. The purpose of observing your words is to get you to be more conscious about the energy – through your words – you exude into the universe. Much like all the other topics previously discussed, there is no way to improve on areas of encumbrance that impede your path to success if you are not aware of your contributing behavior. If you are complaining about a circumstance, it is impossible to understand that your behavior and/or reaction are the very things that can either extinguish or perpetuate your discomfort. You must be cognizant of that which needs altering in order to start the process of changing your outlook, which will ultimately change the climate of your environment.

Here is an interesting perspective Zig Ziglar, the greatest motivational speaker of our time, shared in one of his speeches:

"Most of the people who always seem to have problems fail to recognize that they actually are the problem in one way, shape or form…"

This statement illustrates two things. One, the act of complaining is NEVER useful in the transformation of a setting, situation, circumstance or person that appears to be wrong in the eyes of the complainer. Two, the complainer can't possibly see past the problem that stands before them if ALL their attention falls upon it in that particular moment. Therefore, since you, the complainer, CHOOSE to focus your energy and attention on that which appears to be wrong, instead of that which could be, YOU essentially become the ONLY thing standing in the way of a solution – for yourself or the others involved. The formula for success often requires moving out of your own way. You may have already discovered that this is just about impossible as long as you continue to focus on the illusion of lack, rather than the potential for abundance or resolution. Note: keep in mind that there is no such thing as lack in this Universe that is always unfolding, providing and making itself available to you.

The act of complaining simply implies that you are not ready for the modification that is necessary for the evolution of self – yourself –you so desire to experience. You see, it is impossible to realize or breathe life into your Higher Self (the spiritual placeholder of your true potential) if you spend all of your time worrying, complaining and expressing discontent about your external, physical circumstances. A lesson in A Course in Miracles suggests that nothing in this world has meaning - including upsets involving people, places and environments - other than that which we give it. Giving meaning to all things that occur outside of you is futile and does not support growth, expansion or increase.

It is time to start being grateful for where you are right now. Be thankful for all of the things you have had to go through in your journey, for they are what have brought you to this space, this place and this position of exploration to which you have arrived. Why else would you be reading this book if not for the desire to change course and venture down a path that looks nothing like the roads you have already traveled; to experience things that look nothing like the things you have already been through or encountered.

Your propensity to entertain and express harmful self-talk or criticism about self, and others, demonstrates just how unfitted you are to both comprehend and take the steps essential to making such an urgent shift in your outlook. Instead, you are content with staying exactly where you are. Reflection and a deepened awareness about who you really are will compel you to unveil the truth about the "pay off" received from hearing yourself protest. It could be the perception of being victimized you want people to hold of you in order to create the experience of being unprotected for the sake attracting and interacting with others who love to protect. It could be the position of appearing "right" in the midst of someone else's "wrong doing". It could be the pity, attention and affection you receive from others. It could be the avoidance of having to fulfill the arduous task of living up to higher standards and expectation. Regardless of the reward, it is from understanding the satisfaction you receive from your ingratitude where the possibility of change begins to emerge.

With every challenge that arises in your life comes an opportunity to make a choice that either serves or hinders the process of your progression. Either you can accept, adapt, and accelerate toward a solution or alternative means for resolve and completion; or you can continue to wallow in pity and resist the necessary changes and modifications that will move you past the temporary ordeal. Which do you believe is more advantageous when it comes to attaining your goals or realizing the life you desire? Denying the power to "find the good" in all things despite appearance wastes time, breath and energy that could be utilized to create a much more productive outcome.

Remember: *what you resist, persists.*

You can judge just how much of your energy is put towards being grateful for what is true, rather than what you think is occurring, by asking yourself these questions: Do I demonstrate impatience, stubbornness, irritation, arrogance, procrastination or self-criticism whenever I am confronted with something that displeases me? Do I get angry when I do not receive what it is I prefer? Do I try to force my own desires, opinions and beliefs into situations to manipulate outcomes to work in my favor? Do I have a tendency to rally an audience to listen to me protest when nothing else seems to work? OR…am I able to accept things as they are? Do I try my best to look for the good in whatever may appear to be undesirable? When I encounter upset, am I able to shift my attention inward and contemplate other possible solutions that will empower me, and all others involved, to bring ease and grace to the environment or situation? Am I ever willing to look at the bigger picture and be grateful for what that I do have in this right now moment, such as my income, my home, my health, my family, my dreams…and most importantly, my purpose?

Regardless what is happening in your life at this moment, there is always something for which to be grateful; always a positive element to be found in every event that unfolds throughout your day. As I mentioned earlier – nothing becomes visible until you turn your attention upon it; nothing has meaning other than that which you give it. A positive outlook or outcome to any situation cannot and will not exist until you consciously make a point to become aware of it.

Complaining does absolutely nothing but keep you complacent, infertile and ineffective, right where you are. Zig Ziglar went on to say in his speech, that "nine times out of ten, the person who WON'T take step number one, will also be the person who will not take step number two." Most often the number one step for the complainer (or anyone for that matter) to take would be to silence the negative emotions and thoughts that immediately surface when they are presented with difficulty or opposition. How else can one be enabled to imagine ways to get past a problem? Step number two would be to take action in creating the best outcome for all persons involved, not just for the self. Complainers are usually people who are lazy or have no

131

concept of perseverance. These are usually the people who would find life to be much easier if someone else could do the work for them.

I often tell my clients and listeners that complaining is a form of self-loathing disguised as the comfort with which we swathe ourselves when we feel the need to judge our process and others. Irrespective of which perspective you hold, being disgruntled over a situation or circumstance of which you do not approve brings about very little profit.

Do yourself a favor and look back over the day. Pinpoint the moments where you complained about something or another. Besides the fact that those few moments you spent faulting, accusing or disapproving an event made you feel much better, reflect on whether or not your outcome actually changed as a result of your emotional vomiting.

I am confident that the answer is "No."

The next time you feel like vocally criticizing the moment, remember this: Energy spent on negative thoughts or people generates depletion in your emotional bank account. Hold yourself to this awareness and weigh the costs so that you remain mindful of how and where your currency is being spent. By living a soul-centered, purpose-driven life, your spirit will find ways to renew, maintain or bring increase if ever your account runs low. Through the expression of gratitude for your balance, no matter the amount, YOU become a person that holds authority over what is deposited or withdrawn from the safe deposit box that is your life.

With that said, let's try something different.

Throughout remainder of your day, should you find yourself compelled to complain, contemplate ways with which you can refocus your energy. The key is to do this before another thought passes. Considering you may be used to showing the opposite of gratitude when ill-favored circumstances arise, it may be challenging to bend the momentum of your thoughts toward a positive light and loving energy that supports progress and a healthy state of well-being. It is possible and gets easier with practice. Again, the trick is not allowing negative thoughts to enter your mind. When and if they should happen to make a cameo appearance, do your best to make sure they don't go traipsing aimlessly around your in mind. Don't make the mistake of trying to replace the thought in the middle of their performance. Simply allow them to be what they are without judgment and gently direct them to the "affirmation bin" to receive a make-over. As they exit stage left, make the decision to create a new thought that serves you better and honor yourself by finding something for which to express appreciation. This is how you work on transforming your energy into something much more conducive for progress and fulfillment. If toxic beliefs are prohibited from running amuck in your mind, negative words cannot leave your mouth.

Simply put, the easiest way to monitor your thoughts is to remain in a constant state of gratitude.

I encourage women who possess the proneness to complain to be attentive to the possibility of being victimized by the ego's need to create the experience misery. Ego is a self-centered aspect of yourself that refuses to see you succeed for fear of not being needed or extinguished. If allowed, Ego will keep you swinging on a hammock, supplying you with every reason why you should not try to be more, better or greater than you already are. Thus, your intention should to purify all of your thoughts through the filters of love, compassion, purpose and healing. In doing so you can also allow the sweet hum of life to surround you, while at the same time finding peace and joy, or sharing happiness with others despite contrasting external conditions.

I shall remind you of the Lotus flower, a symbol of strength, enlightenment and purity in the practice of Buddhism. I, myself, find inspiration in how the flower flourishes, even in the stagnant and undernourished conditions of still water and mud; it grows proud, ascending with petals spread wide toward the sky, appearing pure on the surface despite its environment. Why? Because it remains focused solely on its purpose to bring beauty and sweet aroma to the noses of its admirers.

A simple illustration such as this sets an example for how we should carry out our own lives, our own passions and our own beauty as women. Just think about the power that comes with possessing gratitude for the essence of life itself regardless of what may be happening around you. Even further, contemplate the silence that is heard in the Lotus's endeavors to reach fruition. It doesn't complain, grumble or whine about its lack of nutrients. It relishes in its own will and power to remain still in its mission to reach manifestation so that it may in-turn offer shade to cool the mud from which it rose. This is the ultimate expression of gratitude. That said...recognize how gratitude is easiest expressed through your ability to give back to that which enables you to thrive, succeed or see beyond the obstacles that were meant to obstruct your intentions.

You can start living a life of gratitude by rethinking your position in life. Instead of seeing yourself as a conduit for lack, envision yourself being tapped in to every single resource you need to accomplish whatever it is you desire. Also, be grateful for what already exists in your life, even despite feeling as though whatever it is you prefer is slow in presenting itself. Practice Patience. Stand in your power and potential. Do not allow your current reality to distract you from your goals, regardless of circumstance. Use your imagination to help you shed light upon the dreams you hold in your heart. All of this helps your Spirit smile and ultimately enables you to enjoy the journey leading to self-actualization. Refrain from being diverted from the lesson that is meant to champion you into your next step, your next level, your powerful vision. Sometimes we tend to "focus on the finger pointing at the moon" when our attention should be directed to the path leading to the moon or on the moon entirely. Yield to the awareness that the mastery of gratitude is valuable in holding your attention on the path and destination to which your "finger" points.

Here are some words to consider throughout you daily ventures: amongst all that exists and operates in this beautiful universe, there is always an opposite to experience of our experiences. There are always two opposing yet harmonious perspectives of anything that is already present or in the process of becoming. And of the two perceptions or facets, there are a plethora of levels, degrees and states in which a thing, person or environment could be alighted upon.

While in the midst of fleeting thoughts, we may recognize (or label) and possibly covet some things that are considered beautiful, rich, appealing, wise, etc. Yet we are seldom conscious of the fact that the opposite of these attributes exist as well. We neglect to remain in the awareness that it is because such aspects exist that its opposites - ugly, poor, undesirable, and foolish – can also exist. One cannot exist without the other. Again, as above, so below; as within, so without. It is the only way that we can differentiate one thing from another in our human form.

Complainers tend to focus only on one aspect of a situation, person or thing, instead of seeing the whole picture. They don't consider the operational side of what they are experiencing, such as the thoughts, judgments, beliefs, perceptions, projections, and agreements made with or about something in order for the experience to show up in the world of effects in the first place. These are the things that are often times hidden from our view when we stay focused on what really doesn't matter. In this space of judgment (which is really what a complaint is), the contemplation of what someone else may be going through, what past they have endured, or what environmental limitations are present are seldom considered.

Nor do they ponder their spiritual accountability in the creation, contribution or attraction of said experience; they ignore the fact that it is only through the corresponding thoughts they may be holding about a particular circumstance that perpetuated the power of manifestation to begin with; giving them yet another opportunity for growth and evolution if they simply stopped and considered the cause and the effect.

In order to have a more positive aspect about life, create a new mission for your "being" that entails considering things without judgment; seeing the sum total and not just half. See what happens when you at least attempt to view the small as large, the few as many and the poor as rich... I can guarantee you, this will help you become more appreciative for the presence of EVERYTHING that exists in your world – the good and bad; the easy and difficult; the pleasant and unpleasant, etc.

1. Listed below are some ideas I have provided that can help you endeavor a life of gratitude, which will eventually set you on the path of enlightenment, abundance and prosperity. You may even begin to see how reaching higher levels of achievement becomes a bit more amenable and gratifying in the process.

1. Create a gratitude journal. Every day that you have been gifted with life should be the inspiration to write in your journal consistently. List the first things that come to mind for which you are grateful before you start your day. Once completed, set out to maintain the same energy and excitement felt as you penned your list throughout the remainder of your day.

2. Surround yourself with things that make you happy so that you are constantly reminded of the sentiments such as joy, love, peace and balance. This could be anything from rocks, pictures, objects, to colors, plants, artwork, etc.

3. Surround yourself with people you appreciate and admire. It is quite unlikely that you appreciate someone for having done something negative in your life. Trust that what you admire about others is also within you. You can always raise your vibration through the environments and relationships with which you surround yourself. Your relationships and surroundings will either oppose or support you in your journey to becoming. Being in the same space (mentally, physically, spiritually or emotionally) with those you esteem, respect, love and support, raises your vibration exponentially. The higher your vibration and the more you choose to live in it (gratitude, elation, excitement, joy, etc.), the more you are able to attract opportunities for success or fulfillment. The more you flourish in these opportunities, the more confidence you will build. The more confidence and belief you have about yourself, you can better challenge the thoughts that previously extinguished your self-worth. Your ability to create, persevere and triumph will then give birth to gratitude. Gratitude moves you to delve deeper into uncovering and transforming negative beliefs that hinder your progress. ...And the cycle continues.

2. Note: Turn your attention toward the light. Remember the times you felt loved and supported. Strive to strengthen relationships with the people who shared themselves with you for the sake of your well-being. Watch how getting out of your comfort zone and embracing positive influences help you grow

137

exponentially. Take advantage of their presence as they are the beautiful reflections of the good, the beautiful and the wonderful attributes that are the innate aspects of you.

3. Surround yourself with people who make you feel appreciated and give back to them in tenfold. Remember the cycle described above. You will discover that a small expression can be a minor start in the grand perpetuation of gratitude that never stops giving. Trust me...EVERYONE yearns to be loved, everyone wants to feel appreciated, and everyone desires to feel as though they are helping or contributing to the greatness in someone else's life. It's a win-win for all involved.

4. Find accountability partners who can help you keep your conversations positive rather than resentful.

5. Learn to live through your spirit, for it will always direct you to hold the position of love. Thus, you will be permitted to see things under the divine light of devotion and gratitude. Everything you say and do will begin to change.

I close this chapter with two quotes that can be useful in changing your outlook and being more grateful for all people, jobs, relationships, places, money and things that are present in your life at this moment and in the days to follow.

"Feeling appreciated is one of the most important needs that people have. When you share with someone your appreciation and gratitude, they will not forget you. Appreciation will return to you many times." -Steve Brunkhorst

Remember not to forget yourself when you are expressing appreciation and gratitude. The endless cycle of thanksgiving will be the cause for constructive outcomes to flow naturally into the world of effects that is your life.

"Let us rise up and be thankful, for if we didn't learn a lot today, at least we learned a little, and if we didn't learn a little, at least we didn't get sick, and if we got sick, at least we didn't die; so, let us all be thankful." -Buddha

Now...be grateful you have the eyes to read the pages of this book. Be grateful you have the mind to comprehend these words and the will power to make proper choices and decisions from this point forward. Most importantly, appreciate the opportunity, the wisdom, the courage and the strength that empowers you to make your way towards destiny with confidence.

Affirm: Giving up is not an option. Everything I need to overcome the areas of my life that have prevented me from achieving my goals and attaining the success I deserve exist within me. I am worthy of abundance. I am strong enough to persevere when my path gets rocky. Even as I am confronted with challenges, my spirit is centered, my heart open and my mind cleared, so that my awareness remains keen. Thus, I find harmony through my appreciation for all aspects of my life.

And so it is...

Let Go of your But!

"Breathe. Let go. And remind yourself that this very moment is the only one you know you have for sure."

Let Go of your But!

- Oprah Winfrey

The Art of Letting Go

Inspirational Passages

Sometimes, the hardest thing to do in life is to "let go." This usually entails people or things, but most especially past circumstances and events. It isn't always that the thing to which we cling is to be viewed, perceived or experienced as "bad." It may simply be an unhealthy element or contribution to our existence that needs to be removed or altered.

In order to make ourselves aware of what "holding on" to something may be costing us, we must weigh the affects its presence (or non-presence for those of us clinging to past circumstances or fantasies that have yet to reach fruition) is having in our lives. Nine times out of ten we will discover that the very thing on which we hold for dear life is the very thing keeping us from experiencing what it is we truly desire.

Consider this for a moment: How is it ever possible to make yourself available to something greater if you are consumed with keeping what hurts or brings you discomfort at the forefront of your mind? What pleasure do you receive from being a victim to past experience; something that has already ceased to exist? Perhaps the appetite for temporary affinity for misery and sorrow to which you cleave today is worth forfeiting the long-term peace and fulfillment foreseen in your tomorrow.

Understand that most times the actual act of letting go is much easier than overcoming the fear that arises when we ponder our life without said thing, person or circumstance. When we think of letting go, our minds have a tendency to process it as losing rather than gaining.

When faced with this dilemma, try instead to ponder this: Imagine a nickel nestled safely in your clenched fist, palms facing downward. When you open your fist it is safe to assume that the nickel will fall from your grasp. Now imagine the same nickel in your clenched fist, palms facing upward. When you open your fist this time, recognize that the nickel still remains nestled in the center of your hand – freely and undisturbed. EVEN MORE IMPORTANTLY, your hand remains open, free and available to receive all that you truly aspire and desire. Recognizing that there is value in the "nickel in your hand" – no matter if good or bad, it still has made some sort of contribution to your life, depending on your perspective. Hopefully this illustration will enable you to accept things as they are without trying to remove or dismiss them.

Embrace and accept your mind and heart just as they are - perfect, whole unsupportive complete. The key to life is in remembering that thoughts can always be changed and transformed into constructive energy forms. It is in the process of converting your ideas, beliefs, doubts and fears into thoughts more conducive for creating joy and happiness where your experience of life changes. Through your willingness to practice choosing new perspectives and releasing unsupportive thoughts you become empowered to determine what unfolds in your life, and how. Mastering the art of letting go doesn't always mean denial. It may simply entail removing any and all expectation from what you are holding on to in order to remain centered and at peace in the midst of your challenges.

Succeeding and reaching your highest potential is contingent upon on the level of awareness you hold regarding your tendency to be clingy. Your capacity to accomplish your goals or overcome challenges is determined by your ability to let go and live in authenticity. Progress escapes you when failing to accept what is and open yourself to ALL possibilities. Rising above circumstances lies in the power to turn what was meant for harm into an advantage. Let go!

Challenge yourself to contemplate what is or is not contributing to your success or evolution.

Something from the Tao Te Ching:

In pursuit of knowledge,
every day something is added.
In the practice of the Tao (the art of living),
every day something is dropped.
Less and less do you need to force things,
until finally you arrive at non-action.
When nothing is done,
nothing is left undone.

True mastery can be gained

146

by letting things go their own way.
It can't be gained by interfering.

Let go of something today.

Let Go of your But!

From This Moment Forward

*W*allowing in pity, complaining and deeming others as the reason that your life up until this point has not turned out the way you intended will by no means serve you constructively. If you desire to have an existence that looks something other than the one you are currently living then you MUST change your belief system, right now.

Step into the awareness that your life is far from over. In fact, depending on your degree of wakefulness regarding the power to create and manifest – moment by moment, your life is actually just beginning. The fact that you sit there, in this moment, reading these words proves that there is still work for you to do; work that may involve something as simple as getting back on course or as complex as bringing to life a dream that can potentially change the lives of million. How can you move forward if you are not willing to be accountable for your part; for your contribution to how your life has transpired? Trust me, acknowledging even small things such as allowing circumstances or not trusting your intuition can determine the paths we encounter throughout our lifetimes.

Yes, we are all aware of the fact that people or situations arise that can distract us or lure us so far off track that we can no longer remember who we are and what we came here to do. Or, maybe we have been so wrapped up in making sure other people reach their dreams that we never even took the time to figure out what it is we have been assigned to carry out.

Naturally, it really doesn't matter where you are in your journey. The point is that you begin to comprehend exactly what I mean when I say, "there is work to be done." Applaud yourself for having arrived to this moment, for this is an awesome indication that awareness has brought you to the brink of evolution, transition or even transcendence. The responsibility of maintaining and fulfilling the purpose that was intended for you at birth (or possibly before then) is not one to be taken lightly.

Even though there is a major shift taking place in the Universal perception and beliefs people hold about self-actualization and purpose, most people would rather not be bothered with doing the work to see a desired life come to fruition. Being accountable is a huge and commendable step in this process, one that is often avoided or overstepped. There is plenty of reason to be inspired and excited by your willingness to begin taking responsibility for what has happened and what is taking place around you. It is the only way you will be able to be a whole and completely present participant in the remaining portion of your life.

I offer that you take a moment and ask yourself the following questions. Give yourself time to answer in truth and the utmost form of honesty you can possibly express with and to yourself:

What have I been tolerating? Am I allowing others to treat me in ways of which I do not treat myself? Do I perceive and treat myself as something other than how or what the Creator has made me to be? Where and when am I over-extending myself and where am I compromising my own needs for the sake of someone else's? Have I always opted to "take the high road" or make the most next appropriate step toward healing in challenging circumstances, people or situations I encounter, and if not, why? Do I love myself? Do I love other people more than I love my own life purpose? Am I willing to be the reason I can't move on? Am I willing to allow someone else be the reason I can't move into the life I desire to live?

There are million more questions you can ask yourself as a means of deliberating the intricate reasons behind previous behaviors that have hindered you from growth and kept you treading in shallow waters of stagnation...that is, until today. While it is good to focus on finding the answers to these types of questions, you must be careful not to sit and wallow over what it is you discover about yourself. Regardless of your answers, remain holding the vision of your life; remember who you truly are beyond your opinions, perceptions, and judgments. This type of soul exploration is meant not to for you to find reason to experience guilt or shame...this will only keep you sedentary and confused. I merely bring these types of queries to your attention as a means of helping you recognize areas and aspects– some small, others large – of yourself that are out of integrity or alignment. Like many of us, there are instances in your life where the pitfalls encountered along your journey that seemingly caused you to backslide could have been circumvented. They could very well have been avoided. Yes, it is true that the excruciating affliction doled out by malicious and selfish individuals should be accounted for, however the time has come to recognize how replaying thoughts about unfairness and redemption is simply another form of distraction. We must not waste time and energy on things we over which we have no control.

151

At some point they will be held accountable for their own actions, this is none of your business as well. Your business is to stay in your lane and completely be accountable and conscious about how and what you are doing with what happens to you. Another person's choice whether or not to be liable will be of no concern to you the moment you start to re-focus your attention and energies on what matters most to you.

Surrendering to the concept that you are the only person responsible for what occurs in your life. The only relationship you are ever truly having is the one you are having with self/Self. Meaning, anything that happens in your life is a direct reflection of not only you, but also what is occurring within. Thus, taking ownership for how you choose and the outcomes that transpire as a result of your choosing is where your efforts and energies are best spent. Otherwise you will never move past trying ordeals. Instead, you become more susceptible to attracting the same situations; more of what you judge, over and over again.

So...where do you go from here? Great question.

First things first...it is extremely imperative that you do all you can to forgive yourself for allowing external sources to obstruct your path or weigh you down with self-imposed baggage. Regardless of whether or not you perceive yourself to be "right" in your position about current or previous affairs, the objective remains that you are at a point where holding on to certain things, ideas, concepts or emotions no longer serves you. It is in your best interest to focus on moving forward with integrity, self-love, respect and honor. As you do this, be careful not to entertain the concept of leaving one state in order to move into another. Concentrate on moving forward in a manner that is healthy and delightful to your well-being. Leaving or getting out of a situation, environment or relationship carries with it a negative connotation that does not support creating a greater or better experience. Most times we as women have a tendency to do this, still holding on, regretting or despising our previous

152

conditions. Remember, the intention behind "letting go of your buts" is transformation, transcendence and transition. It is your mindset and level of mindfulness that determines what you can potentially create in your next moment.

Simply create the objective to let go…breathe…and move forward.

To do this, you have to let go of things that hinder you from evolution. Take responsibility for the choices and decisions you have made thus far, for it is exactly theses allowances that made room for such toxic entities in the first place. Take charge of who you allow in your life as well. Remove or reassign roles for the people who serve no purpose. Also, free yourself from emotional leeches that do nothing but suck you dry of the essentials meant for helping you heal the wounds, hold the vision and step powerfully and confidently into your dreams.

Everyone in this world has to answer for themselves. Everyone has to be accountable for the world they create.

Waiting for someone else to rescue you wastes valuable time. Build up your endurance, your strength. Start really trusting in your abilities to move past the past. Your friends can't help you. Your parents can't help you…a therapist, pastor or mentor can only help you go so far, but even still, the rest is up to you. Ultimately, you are the only one equipped to do the work it will take to stop the madness and break the cycle.

Here is something that may help you to see how making a change in your position, as well as, your perception of self and individuals who increase or diminish the level of your existence, have affected your path to purpose. I will first reiterate one major factor that we have a tendency to forget in our day-to-day comings and goings. You are not a human being trying to have a spiritual experience. You are a Spiritual being having a human experience. All this simply means is that you must live from the inside out, not the outside in, in order to experience the fulfillment, connectivity, love and passion you so desire. This means truly understanding that life neither works nor works for you when it's lived from your circumstances inward.

With this in mind, do yourself a favor and recall any recent instance where you neglected to remember that you and your Spirit were the co-captains leading team You. What may possibly enter into your awareness is the notion that you have quite possibly been a cheerleader or a substitute player for team Other Than Myself. You have been standing on the sidelines hoping and believing that your day to shine, your moment of glory will arrive as long as you work hard, support your teammates and make your presence apparent in the eyes of the Coach (Creator, Universe, or the God of your understanding). Unfortunately, with this you developed the habit of putting other's needs and desires before your own, and benefiting very little from the high level of effort and energy you consistently offer any and everything in the world beyond you. It wouldn't surprise me if you have also created the experience (once again taking ownership) of feeling depleted, exhausted and walking away from the game injured and disappointed by loss.

Here's a new awareness: How can this be a true perspective if you didn't even participate as and in the fashion in which you were meant? Is the sideline the proper place to partake in competition, or is it on the field, the court, the mat or the ring? Were you even equipped to compete? How well did you nourish and nurture yourself? How did you prepare for your moment of glory? Did you study...eat right...rest well...share your excitement...reflect on your choices...plan or strategize...build relationships...gather information?

Take responsibility as you move forward and into the life you desire, and your experience of the world will begin to change.

What do you think your life would look like if you make the tiny yet momentous modification in your position and perception of what happens in your life? Through living from the inside out you become empowered to shine in all of your uniqueness, talent and skill. The exciting thing about it is you don't have to wait for validation, approval or acceptance. The demonstration of facilitating ownership in your life sanctions your endeavor to help others shine as well, without losing value. Enlightenment reveals that you are not able to help others effectively until your own needs are being met. At some point, following your purpose and passion becomes more important than hoping a passerby has enough discernment to recognize your gifts and abilities. Internal reflection will cause you to question your level of belief or trust in self. The practice of communing and connecting with Divine Intelligence leads to the attainment of wisdom that will make clear to you if and when to surrender to powerlessness without allowing the ego to make you feel weak. So you may as well keep going. When in right mind, there is no such thing as failure; there is only change.

As John Randolph Price states in his book *Angels Within Us*: "Our objective is to enjoy the physical-plane experience without getting trapped in the fog of materiality. This means we are to 'live, love, laugh and be happy' without emotional bondage of fear, guilt, greed and sorrow. Our role in this world is to have everything without possessing anything – to enjoy an all sufficiency of money without being preoccupied with 'making money' to have right livelihood without toiling to make a living, to have wholeness without focusing on the body, to have right relations without selfish emotional affections..."

None of this can be accomplished as long as you remain energetically blocked by frustrations derived from being stunted, playing it small or resisting the innate assignment of living up to your true potential. Letting go of old thoughts, conditions and beliefs is the next most appropriate step to take in attracting greater or better experiences in your life. It is impossible to attain success and fulfillment if you, as a woman, do not first learn how to shift our energy; to learn the difference between being self-full and selfish. Remaining whole and unconditional in your giving - to self first and then to others – is done effortlessly and gracefully from the Spirit within you; from the inside out. Just this effort alone will place you on the path to making better choices and decisions regarding the experiences allowed or tolerated in your life from this moment forward.

Understand that the relationships or environments we maintain also play a large part in how successful we are in attaining the type of life we desire. Thankfully, there are plenty of us who are surrounded by friendships and loved ones who offer a great amount of support for our aspirations. However, there are also people who are not as fortunate. We are powerless when it comes to choosing the family members who raise us from children to adults. Other than removing ourselves from the space of relatives, siblings or parents who may be toxic, there is nothing to be done about the fact that we share the same bloodline with them. This will never change and we are not privy to certain capabilities that empower us to change a person's behavior. All we can do is change our position and alter our perception by not taking things personal.

On the other side of the coin lives the notion that taking the stance of accountability in all relationships maintained, such as co-workers, friendships, lovers, business partnerships, etc., and even the situations in which you choose to engage, determines how quickly you can move on to new, healthier ventures. This is impractical without reflection. It is best to determine what you have or have not learned through each experience in order to gain a full understanding of why you are where you are and why your life has transpired as it has thus far. This may not be the case for you, but there is something to be said about the person who moves from one association to another without first reflecting on or contemplating the reasoning behind its demise, or even why it work out for as long as it did. Usually it is our negligence to assess outcomes that keep us spinning in distress and never-ending cycle of dysfunction, which often times differ in its presentation, but not its cause or effect.

From this moment forward, I encourage you to begin taking the time to sit in tranquility and stillness. Think about many of the instances in your lifetime where an ending came to pass (it's good to consider all circumstances, but more specifically the ones that have brought you any amount of harm or grief that have prohibited you from moving forward). Take the time to breathe in "healing" or at least clear your aura. Allow silence to envelop you in its attempt to reveal mistakes or areas of resolve that could have been considered in previous ventures. Open your mind and heart so that the Universe can make known to you the steps that you will be equipped to take in future experiences as a result of your deliberation. Meditate from the core of your spirit to consider previous steps that worked in your favor, or actions you were able to partake in boldly, with confidence and righteousness so that you may continue to be inspired as you forge ahead in your journey. It is even wise to mull over certain behaviors or deeds committed despite the onset of red flags and/or warnings. Briefly commit to memory all of the choices you made while ignoring intuitions plea. If you look long and hard enough you will start to see what your life may have been had you paused briefly to avoid some of the pains, wounds, scars or disappointments you have endured.

It is okay. Remember, life is not over. You are a step ahead of the game just by being aware.

There is no need to beat yourself up with regret. Regret never moved anyone toward prosperity and the fulfillment of their true purpose. You can be certain that past decisions and experiences will somehow work in your favor as you move into future endeavors, but only if you release them. It is through the intentional act of reflection that you can recognize the true value of a lesson learned. As I have stated in previous chapters, there is an awesome power that is derived from the painful experiences and disappointments of our past. Again, rather than weltering to the weight of dread and pity, be empowered. Tap into the current of despair only as a means of fueling yourself for the road ahead. Suffering is no longer an option now that you understand that the only purpose pain holds is keeping you in alignment with the Creator and your purpose.

Forgiveness is another key essential that will ultimately determine the level of your progression. Forgiving yourself allows you to clear up some of the unnecessary clutter that has kept you captive and disillusioned for so long. It frees up some of the impediments with which you have surrounded yourself as a means of warding off unwanted intruders who threaten to bring harm to your existence. Bear in mind that if you are still bound by mistrust and the need to place blame, it literally means that you are holding on to your idea of what could have been. You have yet to come to grips with the fact that something has ended. Or, you refuse to succumb to the powerlessness you feel as a result of failure. It is even quite possible that you are in the business of trying to maintain power of things over which you have no control, such as the actions and behaviors of people. Thus, you feel inclined to either shut yourself off from or exert aggressive energy onto others. This is no way to live. Your Spirit aspires to be free to experience all the desires of your heart. Your state of emotional imprisonment averts any attempt your Spirit makes to experience itself through you in fullness. Therefore, as long as you remain closed off, your spirit will be dim and be incapable of soaring and reaching its highest level of potential.

Still, your life is not over. There is plenty of time to cleanse yourself with forgiveness.

Let go and let love lead you.

Allow your light to shine…no matter how dim it is in the moment. Allow it to be exactly what it is. Trust that you passion and purpose will eventually reignite the flame. Begin to observe the life that is constantly unfolding before you as a platform for new opportunities. If you don't, you run the risk of someday succumbing to defeat or persuasion that suggests you are not responsible for your own life and outcomes. Stop stumbling blindly in the dark, waiting on your life to be handed to you. You can choose differently. Through self-love, you can choose autonomy. I know you can feel your spirit tugging at you, begging you to turn your attention from the past and onto your envisioned self. You have an opportunity to breathe life into the self you aspire to be if you can forgive the self you used to be and relinquish the belief system you once held. Reach forth and take the first steps onto the avenue of transcendence.

It's a new day. Start at the beginning…a new beginning. Here, in this moment, you are being offered the chance to manifest breakthrough. Here, in this moment, is where you can muster up the courage to demolish barriers through the power that comes with the forgiveness you can now express for yourself, as well as others who neglected to meet your needs. The days of staying in situations that don't serve you or cause you to lose sight of spirit as a result of their own intentions no longer exist. And now, the time has come for you to get back on your horse and gallop back to your own individual path to greatness.

I will say this before I close this chapter: Holding on to the fear that you will make the same mistakes in the future will slow you down. Yes, you may move forward, but it will be at a snail pace in comparison to that which evolves when you begin to trust yourself. If you find it difficult to trust yourself not to fall into perilous trenches in this moment, then you can start by placing all of your trust in the Spirit, the Universe and the Creator. Whatever you do, avoid placing your trust in external sources. Don't get me wrong, there are certain resources that may present themselves in your time of need and may even be successful in helping you attain knowledge, but unless you have trust reserved in bright and high places, none of it will matter. For you will find yourself starting over again. You can always trust that your insight will always lead you to avenues and resources you need in order to advance, rise and soar. This will also keep you from placing blame on other people or situations that have seemingly diverted you from where you aspire to be. Instead, the accountability for self and the guidance of your inner-being will be lead to understand when and where patience can be exercised.

Another awareness to acknowledge is that the only thing you truly need in this world is you. Before you react, repeat these words slowly:

The only THING I truly NEED is me.

In dissecting the statement, I am hopeful that you can understand that I do not mean these words in an egotistical sense. I am not hinting to the notion that you don't need anyone else or any material things in order to sustain life. As you delve deeper into the words of this statement, be conscious of the word need. All the essentials you need to live the life to which you aspire resides on the inside of you. You have heard of the quote that reads, "If I don't go within, I go without." It is within where wisdom, insight, love, strength, stamina, thoughts, beliefs, light, etc., reside. All of these things have been neatly packaged inside of you. It is the spirit that keeps all of these vital rudiments organized and available according to your specific requirements. The things that are not available on the inside of you, such as companionship, knowledge, family, financial resources will still be directed to you contingent upon what you have on the inside of you.

As you move forward, be sure to allow your spirit shine bright and flow freely by showering it daily with clean waters filled with positive nutrients like love, forgiveness and compassion. When showered with muddy waters polluted with doubt, mistrust and blame, your spirit becomes slow to action and lethargic in its endeavor to guide you to paths and doorways leading to evolution. Inspiration seems hard to find while in this state of being. You are now in the business of acting consciously and being deliberate in your intention to bring forth the truth of who you are so that you may fulfill your purpose powerfully.

"The best way to find yourself is to lose yourself in the service of others."

-Mohandas Ghandi

Shift Happens
From Wanting to Being

*T*here comes a point in our lives where the search for meaning, purpose and passion becomes the focal point of our dawns and our twilights. The idea that something bigger than what we may have already witnessed, learned and experienced begins to tug on our hearts, our minds and our spirits. We begin to ponder questions we feel will eventually manifest clues or signs that help us to understand our reason for being here on this earth. The monotony of regiment, the disorder of constant chaos or even the "here today gone tomorrow" scheme of life often has us wondering "is this really it?" We struggle with the concept of going with the flow and place great effort into finding ways to validate our existence. Especially as women, maturation compels

163

us to contemplate any and every way to impress unique footprints along pathways traversed in order to provide evidence of contribution. We want others to know we were here or did something great as we passed through this lifetime. Most of us succeed in this area through the birthing of children and nurturing our families; others do it through their careers, businesses or even by way of artwork or writing a book or two. The point is not in the "how" of our delivery, but rather the "what" within process of creating a legacy for ourselves that transcends generations.

Those of us who are in our later years feel inclined to tamper with evolution by wading in a pool of regret or pondering the woulda, coulda, shoulda moments of our lives. If only we were more mindful, we'd instead of discover the plethora of reasons to celebrate the blessings that were both experienced and remain as a result of our presence here in this physical realm. As we expand our awareness and consciously connect with the power of community, ritual and tradition, we can without question recognize the wonder and excitement of being a woman, a creator – much like the Most High. Often, amidst our arrival to the threshold of transitioning from the first act of our lives into the second, we begin to panic. We find ourselves walking on the brink of fear and negating the notion to trust the simple process of growing, learning and mastering our lives. The suggestion of passing on without being remembered becomes our phobia; a dread of possibly dying without ever having had our say or having the chance to become all that we desired but never had the courage to pursue.

Discounting egocentric individuals who harbor beliefs of grandeur that are borne of chasing transitory possessions and sentiments, all of us eventually arrive to a place in our lives where we yearn for something "more," something substantial or something relative to the big picture – the universal whole of our life and how it contributes to the lives of others. In our blindness and ignorance (not in the derogatory sense), we tend to perceive the "more" that we seek as an entity existing outside of ourselves; something separate and external from their innate sense of being. We perceive that our sense of fulfillment will come by way of an anointed individual or an ominous being that dwells somewhere in the ether. There is an old Buddhist saying that reads: "The way is not in the sky. The way is in the heart." This idea that the same power we believe to be "out there" actually inhabits a space within the confines of our hearts, minds, bodies and spirits is incomprehensible to most. Until today, this may have been the limiting belief that has prevented you from achieving your greatest ambitions and reaching your highest level of potential..

Even when alone and surrounded by all we've attained (the good and the bad, the beliefs we've collected, the people we've met, the experiences we've encountered and endured, the different places we've traveled, etc.) we grow consumed by a void that envelops us from the contours of our body to the innermost core of our being. The world of effects and the belongings we gather tend to make us who we are, which hinders us from being powerful creators of effects through our sense of belonging. As we evolve, we become aware of what our lives really have become consequent to transcending in the low places, clouded by gloom and fog that blinded us from true perceptions. What becomes astonishingly apparent is the understanding that what actually could have been opportunities to explore our innate sense of being through the likes of freedom, peace, bliss, gratitude and surrendering to our true nature, was actually spent surviving, struggling, suffering, succeeding, obtaining and achieving. Being intimately and genuinely connected, loving unconditionally, sharing, learning and appreciating life in fullness starts to feel more enticing than continuing to spend our lives chasing things and finding meaning or validation through external factors that are disingenuous or detrimental to our well-being. The rat race of confusion controlled by the impression of reward and/or punishment no longer appeals to us. As an alternative, we slowly begin gravitating towards actions, behaviors, beliefs and practices that generate cause for something greater than our own sense of survival. The desire to contribute to the bigger picture, an invisible force that unites us all in oneness starts to burn fervently at the depths of our soul.

Some of us arrive to this place of understanding very early in their journey, while others may not reach this epiphany until trauma has brought them to the brink of death or despondency. What I offer is that you remove that you remove the judgment – of self or another – about how long it took. What really matters is you arrived. Now that you know better, you can do better.

Still, letting go of the desire to accumulate affluence, lascivious escapades, accomplishment and admiration for the sake of cultivating spiritual (not religious) values, integrity, peace, meaningful relationships seems daunting and unreasonable. Thus, creating a life filled with happiness, self-actualization, and liberation takes a back seat to our need to build careers, conform to societal standards, maintain facades, or appeal to others on behalf of being accepted.

The whole idea of abundance, prosperity, freedom and peace sounds like mumbo jumbo to most who have been and still are conditioned to believe that life is about suffering and struggle, or running the treadmill of triumph beyond tribulation. After all, "what doesn't kill you only makes you stronger." As true and real as this idea may be to most people, there still exists a possibility that we really have a choice to alter or modify how the our lives, relationships, environments and the world occurs to and for us, in order to have a different experience of life.

Try this on for size:

What ideas pop into your head when asked to consider the possibility of being human or…just being (as in your spirit self in physical form). Meaning, what if you didn't have to place so much effort into gaining and surviving in a place you've been conditioned to believe is a "dog eat dog world"? What then would you hear if it was suggested that all of your qualms of loss, lack and extinction merely exist as a result of thinking small or living in lack-mindedness?

Before you answer those questions, I strongly encourage you to stretch your thoughts. Relinquish any resistance that limits you from really recognizing the possibility that you are the only presence impeding your path to the life you aspire to live

Take a moment to sit still, breath and ponder without hindrance.

What resonates with you when you reflect on the possibility of having harmony, balance, peace and a sense of connection in your life? Do you doubt and dismiss this impulse, thinking that deliberation would make you delusional and unrealistic? What would you actually heard the still small voice saying, "Be the you you've always aspired to be. Follow your passion, live your purpose and share your gifts and unique talents." Would you let go of your need for validation from your peers or remove your doubts and worry of lack, so that you may experience basking in the blissful radiance that comes with fulfillment? Or would you listen to the already-forever-resolved voice in your head that shouts every reason under the sun why you should stay in your lane and carry out that which was assigned to you by society, your parents and your predecessors?

Now, imagine just how much making a small yet significant shift in how you started your day would impact your life. It all starts with your thinking. Feelings and perceptions are perpetuated by the thoughts we allow to roam aimlessly in our head. Change your mind today. Instead of being overwhelmed by the big picture of getting from point A to point B in areas of realization in your life, start small. It is impossible to recreate your thought process or re-condition your mind overnight. Take baby steps. Start from the inside so that you can begin to attract the things in your life that resonate from what you are being rather than what you are wanting or doing. You see, the Law of Attraction/Correspondence suggests that you can only bring towards you all that you are being in this moment. We have this misperception that we should focus on what we want for our lives rather than on what we do not have. Remember, "wanting" is a state of "not having" rather than a state of being. To want something means it ceases to exist or has yet to arrive. Therefore you are actually being without that which you are wanting. Example: There is a different mindset that comes with wanting peace as opposed to being peace. "You can not have something until you are willing to become it," are the words of the esteemed Dr. Michael Bernard Beckwith.

Now, when we shift our perception from what is missing to what we are being, we can start to notice areas of our being that are not in alignment with what we truly desire to experience for and through ourselves. Our focus changes from living life in accordance to what is expected for us to living life in accordance to what is true for us. This eventually brings to light an undying desire to express gratitude for all that we have the pleasure of experiencing authentically. The arrival of each new dawn is welcomed with a fervent "thank you" to the Universe for all that we are, all that we have done, been, and had, as well as, for all that we will become, do and gain. Suddenly, we grow more empowered to move away from the fictitious and impoverished mindset stemmed from feeding our egotistical sense of entitlement. We become humbled in our endeavor to shift the focus of attention off of ourselves and onto the desires of others who surround us. Thereby granting and bringing into existence a greater sense of fulfillment that transcends the self and contributes to the collective movement of love, peace and harmony that we all aspire to experience. And...eventually, we are moved to consider ways with which we can bring more of what we previously wanted into our lives, not for our own gain, but for the benefit of the bigger picture. The more this happens, the more inclined we are to surrender to the powerful presence that connects us to each and every being on this planet. Respect for life in totality then paves way for the allowance of Divine Intelligence to shine brighter from within. Slowly, we become inspired to relinquish the need to have and be more, better or different than what we already are. Thus, we can begin accept and love all that is, exactly as it is.

Dissimilar to what we believe in this moment, all of our truths, concepts and ideas, continuously evolve or change depending on where we are in our lives. As I mentioned earlier, the majority of us reside in a space of exploration, learning and seeking answers to what seem to be compelling life queries, only to discover in later years most of what we thought we required really had very little relevance to who we would end up becoming. Some of us dwell in the space of contemplation, where meaning and purpose for life is sought. And lastly, there are few of us who inhabit the space of reflection where appreciation or regret are spawned consequent to pondering insights we've acquired through hindsight's whisper.

Regardless of position, we inevitably evolve to and through what Dr. Wayne Dyer refers to as the Morning, Afternoon and Evening of our lives. Age is of no relevance in this concept, however most of us subscribe to the assumption that with age comes wisdom. Yet, one can be wise in youth while one can be grow to be imprudent as they progress in years. Still, the process of evolution dictates that whatever was true, valuable and meaningful to us in one period is seldom relevant in another.

Putting into practice the continuous expression of gratitude and acceptance for all that dwells within your awareness creates the room to allow your vision to spread beyond the boundaries of your consciousness. Through this, the conditioned mind that once compelled us to consider ourselves first shifts us toward placing our attention on being selfless and of service to others. We can then begin to contemplate living from a place of virtue, a place of connection and a place of embracing life's process. Best stated by Dr. Dyer, "We cannot live the afternoon of our lives according to the program of Life's morning. For what was great in the morning will be little in evening. And what may have been true at morning, by evening will become a lie."

Over all, the whole purpose of life is to BE happy – joyful, peaceful, and loving. Happiness is the ONLY avenue that grants access to having and bringing meaning into our lives. The pathway to gladness guides and positions us gently toward sharing and giving rather than striving to get from one place to the next, or gaining one thing after another. Being happy obliterates the concept of survival and promotes the principle of being – being human, being spirit, being authentic, etc. The constant determination to be something other than what you truly are, to put effort into making things happen instead of allowing things to occur naturally, annuls your opportunity to simply arrive to the doorstep of your own life. Continuously seeking validation through the attempt to acquire things that are seemingly beyond your reach, or focusing your attention on situations that are out of your control, negates the chance to arrive to a place of blissfully experiencing all that you already are, in this moment.

Sometimes, we are so busy in our quest for doorways, maps and road signs leading to the discovery of our true purpose that we miss what could be standing right before us, or what potential already exists within us. It is important to remember that each and every of one us come from the same exact Source, the same energy field that even before conception, provided us with sustaining essentials that 1)enabled creation, and 2) allows creativity to happen through us. Using nature to exemplify effortlessness, we can be reminded that all we ever need to grow and evolve is already provided from the Source from which we were created. Before we were born, we were fortunate enough not to have to search for our traits and characteristics, our personality, our bone structure or our body. Even the parents that served as the conduits for our existence "happened" without effort on our parts.

Quite simple...everything that we are being in this moment existed before our birth. Everything we needed to become who we are was granted gradually and naturally – not all at once. It was only during the first few months of our lives where we were truly able to "be" authentic in nature without "correction," just before the journey of effort and ambition began. As a result of the having to rely on parents who provide nourishment and nurturing, we inadvertently learn how to be independent. We are reared to take care of ourselves, to become something or someone that "represents" the family well. We lose our natural sense of self by learning what is "right for us" and how to properly express ourselves as a boy or girl. Consequently, we become conditioned to believe what others before us believed. Thus, our provision no longer gets served naturally. It gets provided contingent upon the conditions we choose or choose not to follow. Even before we can speak, we begin to learn the meaning and value of love and fear. Our fear of punishment or lack keeps us doing the all the "right" things in order to be rewarded with love. Here is where our ego takes over, telling us that life without the ambition to get, be and have better, more or different from others has no meaning. Ambition is what makes us teach, and believe, that our self-worth is based on what we have and own. Through this, our lives becomes centered on maintaining our validity with the things we obtain.

As is obvious with the shift that is occurring around the world, this is no way to continue living. We have all been on a hamster wheel of cyclical dysfunction and dis-ease, all centered on the objective of gaining a greater sense of achievement and accomplishment. We start to invent lives and lifestyles that are endorsed by our peers according to "what I have" rather than "who I Am," as we intended the moment of conception. As a result of seeking validation from our parents, peers and society, our ambition evolves into competition. Through our competition with one another we then become focused on building our reputation, all of which keeps our focus on gaining outside attention and external confirmation in order to experience any sense of fulfillment. It is our way of being "right" or "the best" in accordance to how society deems so. We ultimately become more consumed with "living up to" what others have spoken for our lives; rather than listening and adhering to the true calling for a lives that we called forth to make a greater contribution to Universal order.

Perhaps you could rise above "the norm" and follow your true calling. This would involve using your being-ness to give life to Life through creating bliss, goodness, health, love, peace, abundance and compassion. Until this becomes a part of every fiber of your being, you can at least start to understand how the ego has played a part in the "division" concept creates the experience of being separate from your sisters and brothers (physically and spiritually), as well as the Creator. Unfortunately, this is the reason most of us live our lives as if we are alone and on our own; as if all that we need exists outside of ourselves. Our fear of being without is really what stimulates our ambition, rather than the genuine state of being in alliance and alignment with Source from which we came that inevitably keeps us connected to everything for which we search.

Need, as in lack, no longer exists the moment we shift our minds and our thoughts toward the soul/spirit/Self we encompass. By doing so, things and possessions no longer bring us value or self-worth. Life becomes simpler when we pursue essentials such as passion, joy, love, peace, wisdom, solace, spirituality, relationships (with self, with others and with the Source) provision and sustenance. Thus, these essentials are the tools we use along the way as we carry out our journey as we envision. Through this, our outlook of life shifts in a way that empowers our existence and enables us to comprehend the importance of staying in alignment with the bliss of life. None of this can be discovered or put to use as long as we live, act, perceive and behave selfishly.

What thoughts arise when you really start to consider how most of your life has been founded on mistruths? By no means is this saying that everything you know today is to be considered a lie. However, what comes up for you when you start to consider that many of the perceptions, beliefs and conditions through which you experience your life have been based off of "stories" that have been handed down from generation to generation. Of these thoughts, perceptions, beliefs and practices you hold, which of these are borne of your own conscious? What about your life is truly of derived from your own cognizance rather than a consciousness that was developed through what you acquired listening to and watching your parents, role models, ancestral traditions, etc.

Once you can answer this question, you will possess the key that will empower you to "let go of the buts" that hinder you from being what you truly desire. You will have the power to change the story – your story. You will have the ability to shift the concept of worry, fear and lack to that of provision, purpose and passion. You can simply be all that was intended for your life.

Now that you know better, you can breathe divinity into the lives of others by sharing all of your truth, all of your being and all of your gifts.

What an amazing life you can live if you allow the shift to happen.

Let Go of your But!

"The beginning is the most important part of the work."
-        Plato

After the Storm

Reassembling the Pieces of Me

*W*hen faced with tribulation, most of us are completely unaware of the notion that it is how we endure trying conditions that will determine what, when and who we will become when our storm finally passes. This is so because we are more inclined to focus our energies on searching for resolutions based on interpretation and emotion, rather than on what is actually occurring. All this really gives us is justification to blame the "perpetrator" or the cause of seemingly unpleasant situations. Truthfully, inquiring about why a storm occurred and why it appears as though it destroyed everything in its path can serve to be irrelevant if asked in an inappropriate manner. If we are not mindful, our "whys" can perpetuate our "buts."

Some of us are inclined to think the "whys" of our circumstances lend to understanding the purpose or reason for the existence of our storms. Others believe that having answers helps in creating a course of action, or aids in one's ambition to be proactive in re-assembling the pieces of their lives. Giving the accuracy of these concepts, it is crucial that you understand that there is a significant difference between asking "why is this happening and what am I to gain from this experience?" and "why is this happening and what did I do to deserve this?" Though the both of these questions start with a "why", the answers you receive will generate entirely different results.

Whenever answers are sought from the Universe, there is a 100 percent chance that you will receive what it is you request in some fashion or another. With this, you can begin to understand how asking the latter of the two questions will only get you more of the same of what you are already enduring. While the first "why" grants you access to the insight you need to move on to your next level of well-being in a way that is conducive for success, the latter "why" keeps you stagnant and blinded to creating a strategy for survival. This is by no means favorable for your well-being, your growth and evolution, or your attainment of potential lessons. All you will get in the end is a pocket full of frustrations, none of which, as I mentioned earlier, are relevant or vital in the process of weathering any storm.

Being more attentive to the questions we ask while spinning in the eye of the storm is one way to deal with chaos and devastation. We can better overcome the mound of buts that hinder us from moving through fear, doubt and unworthiness. Sitting still is also key in maintaining your balance and keeping your ground. The first thing we feel inclined to do in a crisis is act in a way that changes, modifies or alters our situation by any means necessary. As a result, we aren't really thinking or strategizing or even allowing the process to unfold naturally. We are merely physically and emotionally reacting to something that is outwardly disagreeable to our inner truth at the moment. As extremely difficult of a challenge it may be, waiting patiently and peacefully, breathing, and getting centered is one of the best choices you can make in a time of calamity.

In the midst of your trial lies yet another opportunity to follow the laws and likeness of nature. The next time a storm comes to pass, observe from your window how the wind blows, the trees bend, the rain falls and the earth welcomes the rain. Notice how nothing is acting; everything shifts and moves naturally, always going with, but never against, the elements. Most importantly, be mindful of the non-resistance. At the heart of destruction, everything sits still in wait, even up until the moment of uproot or transplantation.

While you practice stillness in your environment or situation, be aware of the thoughts you have circulating through your mind. Focus on what is really happening, rather than placing your attention on the "why" of what you think is happening. Do something different.

Why...? Because we spend our time looking for reasons to blame or point fingers. We even exert much of our energy contemplating ways with which to seek revenge or counter action. Or, as mentioned earlier, we take the pain of the incident personally and immediately begin arranging a pity party that completely distracts us from the peace that is ultimately necessary for our health, sanity and survival. Keep in mind that none of the aforementioned is done for the sake of loving self. These thoughts are just about as destructive as the storm itself. They perpetuate the damage that arises consequent to your circumstances.

Sitting still in search of ways to maintain peace of mind, entertaining thoughts that are loving and uplifting, and asking questions that are empowering are all difficult feats to accomplish. Yet, it is wise to place great effort into resisting the e-centered desires to find fault, harbor shame and guilt, or wallow in disappointment. If you are not cognizant of the thoughts arise as a result panic, you'll lose sight of the fact that the pain you may be experiencing doesn't automatically constitute a need to suffer. Most of us suffer through tragedy because we are unwilling to or do not have the emotional, mental and sometimes physical wherewithal to determine that we are entirely responsible for the prolonging of our pain beyond challenging incidents. We have yet to learn that holding on to grief limits our capacity to live our lives without hindrance. Thus, fear and anger become the emotions through which our entire experience of life is filtered.

We can start to live in the truth declaring that storms always pass; the light we need to guide us through darkness always shows up; the strengthen we need to persevered and endure is always mustered…if we and when we are patient. It is through fortitude that we can begin to recognize the different stages that enable us, as emotional beings, to withstand trying circumstances in a way that is healthy and especially advantageous to our survival. All of this is crucial in determining how we will live our lives once the clouds have cleared. We must be able to check in, evaluate and identify where we are in the stage of overcoming. These stages include the actual experience, the perception of and about what has occurred, the emotional responses to the perception about what occurred, and lastly, the willingness (or lack thereof) to make a choice or decision that fosters change, and the ability to avail yourself to resolution, repair or resolve. Still understand that all in all, it is usually our outlook or perception about what has and is occurring that influences how we will live out the rest of our day, our life...our vision.

Re-assembling the shattered pieces of your existence isn't easy. Being patient, communing in peaceful stillness, and living through the distracting "what if's" circulating through your mind are certainly useful in your endeavor to jumpstart the process of salvaging the remains of your existence subsequent to your misfortune. On the topic of mending the remnants of our lives after tragedy, Luke 15:8 says, "What woman who has ten silver coins, if she loses one of them, does not light a lamp, sweep the house, and search carefully until she has found it." Here, the writer's inclination is to explain how one is and should be responsible for what has been lost, regardless of the "why" and the "how." After all, we are the keepers of our own treasures. Through interpretation, one can see how this verse also illustrates the woman's house as her body, the lamp as her spirit, while her search to find what has been lost is to be done so through the renewing of her mind.

Keeping this in the back of our minds, let me first point out that contrary to observation, life is far from linear, at least not within the realms of our physical experience. We observe the changes in our lives – past, present, and eventually our future – as sequences of ups and downs, all of which effects how we experience what actually happens in any given moment. If we happen to go through a storm when our resistance is up, we may not experience pain and suffering heavily. Quite the opposite occurs when we are ill-prepared for challenges that surface. I should also reiterate that depending on our state of distress, or our level of peace, we have a tendency to make the mistake of putting other's desires before our own need to heal, forgive or move forward. For centuries, women especially have been the keepers of other people's houses but seldom the keeper of the very house that should be cherished first.

Yet, in order for us to exemplify strength resultant to overcoming tribulation, we feel compelled to carry on with the weight of the world on our shoulders as we build careers, enlighten our minds, raise our children take care of our families, etc. More often than not, the aspirations that once floated in the forefront of our minds get pushed to the wayside. Our hopes and dreams, the pieces of silver for which we steadily search, gets buried beneath fear, worry, doubt, and a sense of obligation to care for the demands others. Nobility without replenishment is detrimental to peace of mind when our passion for life grows dim. When we neglect to ensure we are first self-full (a big difference from being selfish) or completely restored from past experiences we become desensitized to our own vigor for realizing our truth. We start living through a default identity that is dissimilar to what we envision in our hearts and minds. Seldom do we ever stop to heal ourselves, to nurse the very wounds that keep us prisoners of our own pain. All we are left with is a hopeless belief that our circumstances have become who we really are.

Be awakened to the fact that this doesn't have to be our truth. Regardless of what we encounter, to stand in the position of living a so-called "hand that was dealt" is to lose everything you ever worked. Instead of focusing on how your life has unfolded as a result of your tragedy, be encouraged to shift your energies toward lighting the lamp within. You see, it is imperative that you begin to understand that you are not your circumstances. It would behoove you to refrain from perceiving and living your life through your external environments and start living from the home with which you were gifted. Cherish the body that holds the spirit and the mind that empowers you to be creative, willed and indomitable in every sense of your being. No matter how hard your situation is, the best form of healing starts when you begin to get your house in order, so that you can let go of your buts and begin living from the inside out, not the outside in.

Often times, we make the mistake of using our external environments to determine the state of our internal well-being. If everything is in place, we seemingly believe all is well with our emotional and mental states. As mentioned earlier, things have become a way for us to gauge our level of happiness, joy and peace. Thus, the accumulation of accolades and amenities we collect along the way are cherished and protected. All the while, our internal "homes" get cluttered with junk, growing dirtier and dirtier on the inside, while the outside gleams with spoils, trinkets and valuables. This is why we experience such devastation when our "precious possessions" end up missing or broken. Had we been properly aligned, a more attuned sense of awareness would reveal a newfound perception that the more we cater to the propensity to "gain things," the more we lose sight of the value of our own lives. All the while, the treasures we should cherish and guard get tarnished, dusty and unrecognizable. This explains the very reasons as to why, when devastation arises, we feel as though we have nothing left inside of us to help us weather the storm. Still, we remain perplexed and confused on a journey to nowhere, failing to understand that we are lost because we never became familiar with "home". Rather than valuing the pieces of your possessions, consider what can transpire the moment you place emphasis on valuing EVERY single piece of you.

Today, challenge yourself to go within and see just how centering your attention on the lessons born in the midst of tribulation can change your experience. Consider the sense of authority honed as you become more aware of your position as the creator of your outcomes, instead of waiting around for "the next shoe to fall." Here is something else to ponder: renowned spiritual leader, Dr. Rev. Iyanla Vanzant, encourages us to discern whether or not we are holding and owning the stance of student, teacher or the object being used to carry out a particular lesson as we weather our storms. Keeping this in mind as you proceed to your next level of awareness will help you to shift your perception of challenges or problems. You'll be able to observe and experience them from more than one angle. When you are mindful of your attitude, perception and position in what occurs throughout your life, you gain access to the Inner Authority that equips you to make better choices that enhance our chances of survival, maintain our sense of self-worth, minimize the onset of suffering, and ultimately move gracefully into successes beyond our imagination.

Throughout my studies, I have come to learn that there are several layers, pieces or segments of ourselves that should be cultivated, polished, and kept on display on the mantels of our minds as we journey toward self-actualization; especially after a storm. However, piecing together the puzzle of our lives can be tricky if we are not equipped with the right ingredients with which to do so. In order to withstand tough times without getting lost in the pain, while still maintaining a sense of purpose and fulfillment, can be a difficult feat if our attention is pointed in the wrong direction.

While speculating over the "ten pieces of silver" mentioned earlier, be encouraged to delve deep within to discover which parts of you could use a little cleaning, refining or protection. This is not only useful while embarking upon a life of completion and wholeness, but also very constructive in growing more mindful of the strengths or weaknesses that impact your ability to earnestly and fearlessly cope through trials and hardships. The art is in piecing your life back together in a way that allows you to clear the space before you so that you can make proper use of your new found courage; so that you can follow your purpose and passion; so, like the lotus, you can rise from muddy turmoil and blossom into an open, beautiful aromatic flower.

Remember the words of Robert Frost: "The best way out is always through."

Compassion, integrity, intention, purpose, gift, talent, passion, love, strength and wisdom are ten qualities of your being that can be nurtured regularly in order to live a life that is enriched and enlivened, in spite all that you've prevailed. When you place focus on these facets of life and your being regardless of injury and circumstance, it is impossible to walk away from any ordeal empty handed. Your life may have been significantly altered, or you may have even been maimed in the process of "going through," but as long as you are aligned with the essentials listed above, the lessons, vigor and guidance necessary to expand and rise above adversity can never escape you. No matter your surroundings, you are charged with allowing your divine light to surmount the wreckage and remnants of deceptive destruction in order to move into the next stages of your journeys. The insight and harmony attained consequent to applying these traits can be paid forward into the lives of others.

You see, the truth of the matter is that you cannot help anyone else find their way through dark times if you are lost yourself; if your own light is dim; or if the most valuable pieces of you are buried beneath the residue of calamity. Some of us carry on with life without a second thought, forgetting or neglecting the process of restoration and the impact it could have on the life we choose to live once the sun begins to shine. This is the very reason why we have a tendency to search aimlessly in the dark for comfort we feel will come from external sources and things. Because we have no concept of accountability, we neglect to contemplate the possibility that the guiding light for which we've searched has always indwelled within.

Loving, healing and trusting yourself must become your first priority if and whenever you find the time to sit in peace and reflect on what has transpired. Balance your life out by reading, praying, meditating, exercising, learning, and lifting your spirit with delight. Begin by perceiving difficult times as opportunities to experience life from a place of creation that mimics the Creator who created you as the paramount masterpiece in your world. Use your time of healing to teach what you need to learn and inspire others around you by being an divine demonstration of peace. Eventually the perception of your "suffering" will shift to one that encompasses compassion; not only for yourself, but also for others who have and are going through the same circumstances you've already endured. Instead of worrying about things you have no control over (after all, what's done is what's done and can't be changed), you will become more engrossed in the desire to help and be of service to those who may not have the strength to carry on in the same manner. Consider making and keeping new agreements that move you towards happiness, joy, peace, tranquility and abundance. Position yourself as victor, teacher, and leader – even if only in your own life. There is power in the simplicity of being and appreciating what you are, where you are and how you are – just as you are.

Contrary to what you may have believed while in the midst of your storm, if you follow your heart, passion and purpose, you will inevitably flourish into a being who is content with refunding the Universe with your radiance, love and gratitude. As you surrender to the pain and embrace the gratification, you will ultimately discover that the key to living the life you've always imagined is in giving from where you have been and what you have been through. This makes the experience of your life all worthwhile.

"Kind words can be short and easy to speak, but their echoes are truly endless."

\-   Mother Teresa

Jumping Hurdles

*H*ow can you start to transcend the hurdle of "buts" that prohibit the physical experience of having all you imagine in your mind? Great question! For starters, at any given moment you feel compelled to utilize the conjoining word "but" between a possibility and an excuse to justify your shortcomings, mistakes and failures, it is wise to consider your true self; the Highest part of yourself that is more inclined to flourish if you could just...allow.

Next, is to understand that the sparks of ambition and dreams you envision are, without reason or excuses, planted within you for a specific purpose. Goals, ideas, concepts simply stay in dormant wait of being made manifest into your external existence through your plans and actions. To the degree in which you are able to recognize your accountability in the unfolding of your preferred experiences is the degree in which they will come into fruition as they are visualized in your mind.

Often times, our lives lack the joy, balance, peace, happiness or sense of fulfillment for which we yearn because we have neglected to live deliberately, on purpose and in alignment with our truth; to do what we must to breathe life into every aspect of our being – spiritually, physically, mentally and emotionally.

Why is this?

Much of this has to do with our beliefs, our thoughts and most importantly our behaviors – many of which were handed down from generation to generation. Again, very few of the thoughts we entertain are originally rooted in our own individual consciousness. Dr. Wayne Dyer suggests that if we "change our thoughts, we can change our lives." In order to do this, we must first be able to discern which of our thoughts need changing and for what reason. Meaning, it is imperative to identify whether or not the thoughts that prompt our decisions, choices and actions are in alignment with the overall purpose of our life. We need to recognize if they are negatively or positively impacting our lives or if they are cause for construction or destruction in the intentions we set.

The easiest way to overcome your "buts" and start living your truth is to be willing and open to change your mind. You can do this by:

- Determining whether or not your thoughts and beliefs really yours or if they have been handed to you from your parents, peers, teachers, friends and lovers?

- Understanding that the real question isn't whether or not your beliefs and values are "right", but rather if your beliefs and values are right for YOU.

  Note: You can determine this by recognizing if they actually contribute or hinder you on your path to success and fulfillment? According to renowned author and teacher Deepak Chopra, the average person thinks approximately 65,000 thoughts per day. Of these, 95% are exactly the same thoughts that passed through our minds the day before, and the day before that, and the day before that... This concludes that only a small percentage of our thoughts were originally ours to begin with. How authentic can our lives be when this is the case?

- As you begin to discern what is "right" for you, practice new ways of thinking, behaving and acting accordingly. Negative self-talk stems from listening to ideas and concepts that are no longer serving you. The more you practice living and being in truth, the more you can minimize negative criticism and judgment. The less disapproval and conviction you have crowding your mind, the less inclined you will be to make excuses or doubt your potential for greatness. You can simply be.

What it means to live authentically:

Living authentically means having the confidence to sing your own song, dance to your own tune and beat your own drum, despite what others may think about you.

Living authentically entails removing the masks you portray to the outer world, so that you, and others, may discover and experience who you really are.

Living authentically involves accepting the "likes and the dislikes" you may have of yourself, so that you may begin to own your power to thrive in and with all of your unique talents, gifts, skills.

Living authentically means being free to create the life to which you aspire, regardless of how ridiculous it may seem to your family, friends, peers and loved ones.

Living authentically means making yourself available to possibility rather than hiding behind the doubts, fears and thoughts that hinder our growth and evolution.

Living authentically means finding a way to love yourself completely and without inhibition.

Living authentically means having unwavering strength and courage to simply be.

Living authentically means being open to the flow of goodness and compassion instead of being afraid to love and help those in need through your gifts and talents.

Living authentically means selflessly allowing yourself to be the gift you were meant to be for others.

The Four C's

Here are a few concepts and/or actions I like to call the "Four C's" that can be useful as you begin practicing letting go of excuses that hinder the process of getting re-acquainted with your true self. This model will ultimately steer you back on course to fulfillment and on your way to surmounting the "buts" and obstacles that have impeded your success until today.

- Complaining

Recognizing your tendency to complain is another way of bringing to attention those ill-favored characteristics of situations, environments, and of course, the self. It serves you nothing to fester in discontent. The moment you feel the need to grumble, stop and take the time to honor your feelings. Breathe through them and ponder ways you may move beyond your feelings into your preferred experience. Your choice to be accountable for the situation, no matter who's at fault, directs you to a place within where resolution and/or healing for everyone involved can be revealed.

- Comparison

Be careful about being envious of what others are or what they possess. Instead of begrudging another person's life or property, turn your sentiments into the inspirational fuel you need to attain exactly what you desire and deserve. Understand that such emotions centered on jealousy are meant to shine light on talents or abilities indwelt within you. Recognize that what you admire in others, you also possess. It is your responsibility to courageously find your way to the path that will enable you to become what you see reflecting back to you from another. The only reason you recognize it in others, is because you have yet to see it within yourself. What you admire about someone is your desired self personified showing up as a glimpse of what's possible and true for you. Respect yourself enough to master the art of admiration constructively by becoming that which you admire. Instead of comparing, be compelled to create the highest version of yourself imaginable.

- Compromising/Conforming

Following conditions and beliefs that were inherited rather than those which are self-cultivated will eventually lead you to a life filled with regret. The frustration, anger and depression you encounter when reflecting on your circumstances and choices are ways to determine where and when you are compromising your true self for a false, masked version of an individual seeking acceptance. You can always know when you are conforming by observing your actions. How much of what you are doing or being is done in an attempt to fit in or avoid "rocking the boat" in relationships or situations? Nine times out of ten, we as women tend to ignore the signals that tell us when we are in or out of compliance with in-authenticity. Opting to use inner authority to live in our power becomes inconsequential. However, the question you could begin to ask is this: Is the act of sacrificing my own happiness and fulfillment worth the mountain of "buts" that will keep me from being all I desire to be? Is the act of conforming to traditions and beliefs really worth forfeiting the life for which I yearn?

- Change

If you are like most people, the word change stirs up feelings of anxiety, worry, dread, loss of control, and apprehension about the unknown. Yet, it is the only thing that is constant in our time/space reality. Confronting your fear of change enforces growth, healing and success. Your greatest objective is to overcome the fear so that you can live life completely present mentally, spiritually and physically. The best way to embrace change is to accept things as they are and to focus on providing yourself self-care and in every single situation you encounter. Minimize the distractions that obstruct your view from seeing all that is possible in the midst of change. Begin to live your days as simplistic as possible so that you are always prepared to make the most loving and efficient decisions and choices. The experience of chaos in the midst of a calamity that uproots change can be reduced with clarity.

Today, I challenge you to re-introduce yourself to the real you, so that you may start to live life deliberately and by design. Here are some suggestions to get you started:

- Know who you really are; know your purpose and your passion.
- Determine whether or not you may be compromising your life in order to attain validation from others.
- Take a hard, honest look at your patterns, beliefs and habits to determine whether your actions and lifestyle

are in alignment with the person you envision or aspire to become.

- Establish whether or not your behavioral life and your public persona fall in line with the values, beliefs passions, desires and visions that define your authentic self.

- Use your complaints to your benefit; See them through to a solution

- Honor your gifts, talents, strengths and weaknesses

As one chooses the path of living in authenticity, one tends to be more inspired to partake in meaningful work and service, cultivate great relationships and resources, and surround themselves with all things good, healthy, beautiful, supportive and productive in nature. All of this contributes to confidence that is gained when life begins to unfold – step by step, moment by moment – as visualized in the mind. True accomplishment is the greatest form of inspiration.

In closing this chapter, I will leave you with this quote from the Tao te Ching scriptures. It is my hope that this will jumpstart you into finding the audacity to relinquish false beliefs, thoughts and actions; discovering the beauty and freedom that comes with living authentically; and inspiring yourself, and others, to get over the hurdle of buts and start living your life as it is meant.

Knowing others is intelligence, knowing self is true wisdom

Mastering others is strength, mastering self is true power

"Pet names are never recorded officially, only uttered and remembered. Unlike good names, pet names are frequently meaningless, deliberately silly, ironic, and even onomatopoetic."

\-   Jhumpa Lahiri

Namesake

*H*ave you ever really considered to what are you actually answering when someone utters your name throughout your day-to-day comings and goings? Are you instinctive with your impulsive reaction of turning of your head when you hear the all-too-familiar sound of a moniker you've owned since the day you were born? Or are you hesitant, timid or resistant when you answer, fearing that you are in "trouble" or being beckoned to come from behind the mask you portray to the world? Perhaps you are confident, deliberate and purposeful with your reply. Either way, I offer that you contemplate whether or not you ever make the attempt to be consciously present and aware of who and how you are being in your life, as it relates to your name? Or…is your name…just a name?

If you are like most people, these questions may seldom cross your mind consequent to the ten million things you have to think about just to "stay afloat" in an ever-expanding sea of responsibilities and life challenges. Yet, if you ever took the moment to stop and deliberate over these types of self-examinations, you just may discover that your whole perspective of life could flip completely upside down. You may also ascertain an conspicuous truth behind your shortcomings and excuses. Simply put…who you are and how you acknowledge yourself has everything to do with your experience of this world.

This is the very reason it is important to cultivate the frequent habit of remembering who you are. This entails recognizing the duality that comes with the word "remembering." One – of course, is what we do whenever we have forgotten or misplaced a thing, place, person, date or concept. But then there is also the re-membering that comes with getting re-acquainted with yourself, the self that existed well before you were "formed in the womb." It involves allowing your current self to join together with your intended self so that the physical experience of your deepest desires can experienced in physical form. As Neale Donald Walsh states in his book, *Conversations with God*, "The goal of your life is to seek what is Truth, Love and to recognize, re-member, find, choose, create, become and make the experience of who you are and want to be."

Most of us have grown accustomed to thinking that if we work hard to reach our goals and overcome our obstacles at all cost, life will turn out grand in the end. To some extent, this is true. On the other hand, if we never stop to remember who we are, how will we ever know if we are heading in the right direction, healing our wounds, forgiving others, making the right choices or even living the life that was meant for us? The effort to attain self-realization is extremely commendable, however, what good will it do if in the end our sense of fulfillment, or the opportunity to recognize our intended self in physical form was never realized. I mention this over and over again in my writing: There are many people in this world who die with their song (gift, talent, passion, mission, purpose, etc.) still inside of them. Many "successful" people have reached an admirable level of affluence, only to be left discontented consequent to never having (or taking) the chance to follow their own passion, or their own purpose. They never took the time to remember who they were on the inside.

One of the easiest ways to undertake the inordinate task of "re-membering" is through aligning yourself with the power of your name – first name, middle name, last name, whole name, whatever the case…it doesn't matter. You must recognize and maintain the validity in your name…it is yours, and no one else's. Despite the fact that someone else may share your name, the identity that comes with it is entirely different. Your name uniquely establishes the fact that you are here; that you exist. Not from an egotistical perspective, but rather one that enables you to understand the significance of your donation or contribution to balance, harmony and evolution of our world, our people, our planet – our Universe.

However, remembering who you are, through your name, is the first step to creating a shift in how the world occurs to and for you; to getting over the hurdles of "buts" that stand before you and the finish line; to attracting like-minded individuals that support the vision you hold for your life; and to establishing your "rite of consciousness" as continuously unfolding. If you don't know the literal or self-appointed meaning of your name, how then can you be aware of what you are actually answering to whenever your name is called? Are you instinctively giving your attention to utterances that merely sound familiar, or are you actually responding to a unique implication that you inherited from your parents on the day you came into this world? If any of this sounds familiar to you, it's no wonder you have a hard time letting go of your but! How else can you rise above challenges and obstacles if you can't even conceive of the power you possess just by standing in your I AMness? Can you not even recognize the beautiful wonder that comes when considering the idea that you even exist at all.

I am reminded by the awe-inspiring lyrics of *Holy Now*, by Peter Mayer as he sings about his spiritual upbringing in comparison to the revelation of Spirituality and Awareness developed in his more mature years. He says:

Wine from water is not so small,

But an even better magic trick

Is that anything is here at all

So the challenging thing becomes

Not to look for miracles

But finding where there isn't one.

In honor of the Creator, the first miracle to be acknowledged is that this world even exists at all. The second miracle to recognize is that YOU exist. And you don't just exist; you are a powerful and dynamic component to your life. Without you, your life cannot happen. So why not show up powerfully, uniquely and indisputably.

Imagine the possibility that your name is a lifeline to riches, wealth, intelligence, courage or perseverance that has been accumulated through ancestry; or what if you are chosen as "the one" to leave behind a legacy or an empire that will allow your descendants to live a life of fortune, edification, creativity and artistry. Now imagine your life if you were to become conscious of such prominence that comes with bearing your namesake. Continue to speculate over the possibility of forfeiting these possibilities consequent to being unaware. Are you able to recognize the two different ways of being and living in such a small shift in perspective?

How are you choosing to show up?

Here is another viewpoint to conceptualize: your name is the signature on the contract between you, the Creator and your parents that was arranged before you said "yes" to the deed of making your big entrance into the physical realm. You answering to the call of your name implied that from that moment forward you would uphold your end of the agreement to always stand in integrity; to always choose peace, love and compassion to self and others; to reach your highest potential and master the art of being you by adhering to the images, signals, impressions, messages and guidance from Divine Intelligence; to grow up wise, mature and conscious in your state of being while here on Earth; to bring to into existence everything your heart desired. Why? Because the desires you possess are the seeds that were planted in the soil of your agreement to essentially provide you with a reason for being. Now as the agreement was placed tightly and safely into your heart, you heard the soft whisper of: "These desires are the mile markers for your journey to oneness, that when followed, will lead you to the realization of your Highest

Self. Go forth, and make me proud. Live in integrity, create what you can, and never give up or let anything stand in your way of having what you – WHAT I – want. "

The question that remains to be answered is: Are you living up to your end of the bargain? Are you allowing excuses to keep you from being who you are really meant to be? What meaning are you giving your life as you continue to evade the responsibility of living up to your namesake?

The attractive factor about living, being and acting from these perspectives is that you don't have to start from scratch. You don't have to be reborn or go through an entire "second coming" process just to stand in the power of your namesake. You don't have to start picking new parents, choosing families, selecting personality traits, electing when you will or will not enter the world... You can start afresh right where and how you are. Right here, right now.

The Creator has provided you a body with which to use and preserve as you carry out your purpose from this moment forward. Your parents, whom brought you forth, regardless of how well of a job they accomplished in nurturing you throughout your upbringing, have already carried out their purpose for existence. What about your part? Here is where you begin to ask yourself: Am I doing the same things over and over and expecting a different reality? Am I really being accountable for what occurs in my world, my life, or my relationships? Am I living up to what my name says I am? Am I fulfilling my end of the contract?

Marianne Williamson, an internationally known speaker, author and spiritual teacher writes in her book *A Return to Love - Reflections on the Principles of A Course in Miracles*:

> Our deepest fear is not that we are inadequate. Our deepest fear is that we are powerful beyond measure. It is our light, not our darkness, that most frightens us. We ask ourselves who am I to be brilliant, gorgeous, talented and fabulous? Actually, who are you not to be?

...your playing small does not serve the world. There is nothing enlightened about shrinking so that other people won't feel insecure around you."

We have become so fragmented as a people, a society and a world consequent to advancement in technology, that most of us have become very distracted and disoriented. Re-membering self and living up to one's name is a tradition that has been saturated by egotistical practices and materialism. As a result, we have created a bad habit following other people's footsteps and pathways that were not meant for us to begin with. We conform and live our lives disjointed from our reason for existence; we listen to our ego's selfish intentions while neglecting to tap into the underlying current of strength and resilience that says "I CAN" or "I AM here for a reason." Instead, we grow consumed with anger, frustration and disappointment when we feel that people are not living up to our expectations or honoring our truth - a truth of which we ourselves are not quite certain to begin with. We are so quick to dismiss people when it appears as though we have been disrespected; so hasty in moving on to the next person, venture or circumstance without stopping to contemplate the impact of our waywardness. All the while, we continue neglecting to remember that if we were truly honoring ourselves, there really isn't any need to sweep people or circumstances out of our lives and memories. We simply need to remember our name. Thus, we can grow centered enough to refocus on what we stand for in our own lives, without having to wait around on other people to act in accordance. Remember, it is ultimately our choice to follow, answer to, allow or disallow that which aligns with or is out of alignment with our purpose, passion and divine inheritance.

Understanding your name gives you power. It is the very reason why some people change their names as they mature in their process of evolution and growth. That way, the name to which they respond matches perfectly to who they are, as well as, who they intend to become. Create the possibility of bringing meaning to your name on your own in the event that one has not been assigned. Doing this equips you with the mindset to be present in the act of re-membering, and prevents you from searching for meaning outside of yourself, in the world. It is what will help you find your song, your gift, and your inspiration. A powerful namesake helps you remember your position in the collective contribution of goodness that says you are courage, wisdom, peace, love, kindness, peace and compassion. It paves a path toward a legacy of your choosing that says you were strong, brilliant, talented, inspiring and magical. Truly answering the call of your name – your life - says you agree to be triumphant, victorious and fully capable of creating and overcoming any and everything that comes your way.

To the degree:

To the degree in which you accept that you are here for a reason is the degree in which your experience of life will be delightful.

To the degree in which you understand and accept your highest level of value, worthiness of for goodness and abundance is the degree in which you can relish in, rather than resent, the workings of the world around you.

To the degree that you recognize and remember your own substance and inner authority is the degree in which others will respect, observe, admire, reward, uphold and respect you.

To the degree in which you understand and live up to the power of your name, is the degree in which the Universe will conspire to match or magnify that which you uphold for yourself.

Remembering who you are helps you cultivate your synchronistic contribution to the collective harmony of community and fellowship. It is in your capacity to resiliently traverse the
206

sometimes-sweet-sometimes-bitter-yet-harmonious wave of life that will change your experience of the challenges and hardships you encounter along the way. Again, if you unwilling or do not remember who you are, how then can you expect others to do the same? I once heard a wise man by the name of David Ault say, "If you don't tell yourself who you are, someone else will."

Now ask: What's my name?

"There are only two ways to live your life. One is as though nothing is a miracle. The other is as though everything is a miracle."

-        Albert Einstein

Living Right

From But to Self-Actualization

Self-actualization is a choice. It is a choice to continuously strive throughout our daily agendas to make evident the person we perceive ourselves to be on the inside. Usually, this involves a series of undertakings that are difficult for most to carry out, especially if one has yet to become attuned or aligned with the purpose for their existence. As we go cruise throughout our days, months and even years, most of us remain completely unaware of whom we really are at the core of our being. Contrarily, it is such knowledge of our unique and individual truths that would make the manifestation of an envisioned self a lot less complex than most may believe. It simply takes a certain amount of diligence, inner communication and a commitment that only the passionate and strong-willed are equipped to exercise. It takes focus, perseverance and extreme patience.

Is this you?

I always like to offer my clients an insight that gives them a different perspective of how the world occurs around them: The life you desire doesn't just happen and you simply don't arrive to a place of abundance, success and prosperity by chance. It takes practice – the practice of being exactly what you aspire to experience.

Here is the key that most of us tend to lose along our way to endeavoring completion: While on the road to fulfilling a life aspired, it is just as crucial that you place great effort into cultivating inner growth as you do with nurturing personal growth and attainment. Even in recognizing that this alone is a recurring assignment we must tend to daily – realistically, moment by moment, there comes with it the challenge of simultaneously maintaining this alignment of the two planes of existence.

To do this, staying attuned to the truth that resides within is vital. As you exceed the different levels of consciousness and/or awareness of your utmost potential, investing the time to reflect and stay in partnership with your authentic self is a great idea. I offer that you release any resistance you may have for reflecting, sitting still and silent or checking in from time to time. Listening with an inclined ear or delving deeper within for Spirit's will enable you to decipher what is "right" from what is "wrong" for your life.

210

How will I be able to distinguish the difference? you may ask.

Remember, whatever lives inside of you will certainly manifest itself in your outer world. Whether it entails attracting the things that line up with what you believe to be necessities, or offering yourself for the service of others, being mindful of your feelings, beliefs, thoughts and desires helps with comprehending what occurs in your surroundings. It also helps you discern whether or not you are living in accordance to the conditions and belief systems that have been engrained in your mind by figures of authority, peers or family throughout your previous years.

Living harmoniously with your truth and in accordance to what feels "right," will not only aid in carrying out your life in a moral sense, but rather, it will also enable you to gauge the distance between who you are now and the self you have envisioned since you first understood the concept of future.

It is your thoughts and ever-expanding imagination that helps you envision steps and pathways leading to your highest potential, but it is your feelings and emotions that serve as the "intention compass" you are to follow in order to reach wholeness and completion. It is the act of paying attention to how you feel about your life – including your surroundings, your relationships, your endeavors, goals, behaviors and physical being – thus far that will propel you forward, as well as, determine the pace and fashion in which you proceed. You will also be more inclined to make choices and decision that are less detrimental than those you may have already made.

In order to fully ascertain feelings and emotions that may arise in your pursuit of achievement (mind you, this also entails the countless times of backsliding and regression prevailed along your path to success), you must understand and know who you truly are at the core of your being. Identifying your truth and understanding the importance of maintaining this truth allows you to move into realization as a whole or complete individual; it enables you to recognize areas of release or modification so that you can be effective in your progress. Thus, honoring, trusting, appreciating, accepting, cultivating and continuously connecting with Divine Intelligence, who made you perfect, whole and unique just as you are, will eventually and naturally become a way of life.

Again, the objective is to get you to understand the impact of living in compliance with what you aspire to achieve, both in spiritual and personal endeavors. Using an emotional compass is the easiest way to stay on course and mindful of the decisions and choices that will help you do so.

I encourage you to fully grasp the information above before you proceed, especially if you are one who has spent a greater part of your life living in accordance of what someone else thought was/is "right." Keep in mind that it is not necessary to judge the fact that you were/are following someone else's map. It is all you knew to do…until today. However, it is important that you begin to understand you have the opportunity to make the choice to take a detour simply by asking: "What is right for me and the life I aspire to live?"

Let's discuss why it is imperative that you approach your journey with the intention to of making decisions that are "right" for the life your Spirit seeks to experience through you – Its vessel. Every being on this planet is amazingly distinct in our mission of fulfillment. Though we are all energetically connected to one another, the intended experiences and paths we take to ascend towards our highest aptitude are completely different. Aside from abiding by traditional rules, regulations, standards and conditions set by society, we often have a tendency to confuse admiration as inspiration or an invitation to follow the footsteps of those who have already attained that which we desire on the inside.

This too is common. As mentioned in a previous chapter, it is what makes us human. Yet, at some point, we must endeavor to be an example instead of being one whom follows the example. If we open and avail ourselves to Divine Flow, opportunity for this is offered to us moment by moment.

One of the greatest revelations I've learned in my studies is that the emotion (energy) of envy can serve to be either a destructive or constructive force, depending on how it is used. I will reiterate that in most cases, coveting what another has gained blocks gifts and provisions we are meant to accomplish, achieve or attain. This is due to the allowance of festering energy, which only causes stagnation and breeds negative sentiments such as doubt, resentment and frustration about your failure to achieve your own desires – which in this case looks exactly what so-and-so already possesses. It doesn't take a philosophical protégé to comprehend how these types of emotions move us away and distract us from our own success, goal or purpose. That is, until one discovers how to use the emotion of envy to spark their own passions and be inspired – through the example that stands before them – to fulfill their own purpose.

Contemplate this for a moment: Have you ever noticed what happens when you make choices based on the input of others or what has transpired in the life of someone you hold in high regard? Have you noticed how things either don't work out the way you envisioned (as illustrated through an external example of one you may have idolized) or you just don't feel emotionally connected to your venture? You may have even felt apprehensive, hopeful, afraid, doubtful or even aggravated when obstacle after obstacle continued to fall before you. Or what about spells in your life when you know exactly what you need to do to get to where you need to go, only you just can't muster up enough excitement to get going. Well…this occurs because you are out of alignment or integrity. You are not following your truth or your passion. You are following someone else's truth, which may ultimately mean that you have your eyes focused on the manifestation rather than on the mystery of "going through" your own process.

We want things NOW.

As a society, and especially as women, we tend to want cookie-cutter examples, formulas and recipes to follow to get cars, houses, status, etc. What about the purpose behind your motivation? Is what you desire to attain all for selfish gain? Or, do you want "things" so that you may somehow evolve into a bigger piece of the universal puzzle that naturally falls into place consequent to heartfelt pursuit. An esteemed woman once told me, "Don't pray for things and money just to have it for show or to fulfill a specific but temporary need. Avail yourself to abundance so that you may become the fullest, most powerful and creative expression of the Most High you can possibly be."

Maybe it is time to start considering which may be most rewarding for you – the quick and easy hustle or the timeless journey of becoming YOU.

On the other hand, think about previous occasions where you followed a passion, a dream or a goal and everything fell into place without as much effort as you'd intended to exert. Resources and people became available without much coercion; avenues and doorways opened the moment you stood before them. Perhaps, the success and achievements you visualized reaching came about much sooner than you anticipated. This is how life unfolds when you follow the Universal Laws of Cause and Effect, Attraction, Correspondence and Mind Action. The cause is your mindset that compels you be accountable; to be completely responsible for physically bringing to life the desires of your heart - your Spirit. The effect...well...your life will simply unfold as it should. When your resist abiding by these laws, your life becomes choppy, dissected, filled with ups and downs, confusion and frustration. Why? It's simple...because you are trying to live a life without purpose or passion. This is not to say you will never face difficulties or challenges. However, the mindset one must have to bring dream and desires into fruition is beyond powerful and focused enough to override or minimize false perceptions that distract you from Truth.

I once heard a man say, "Life unfolds in spite of you, not because of you." What he implies through this statement is that no matter how many detours you take, no matter how many obstacles fall before you, no matter what conditions appear to be insurmountable in the moment you experience them, life will still unfold with or without your participation. Don't misconstrue this to mean life continues whether or not you are dead or alive. What he means is that all things will eventually lead you back to what is "right" for your life in order to carry out what you intended at the beginning. What takes so long for things to unfold for us often times has much to do with our need to be in control, impatient, stubborn, close-minded, and the tendency to follow pathways that are not uniquely designed for our distinct journeys. Thus, obstacles that create pain, discomfort and distractions become the temporary detours we must eventually endure in order to learn lessons. Sometimes it is the only way we become better suited for the road ahead.

So...if it takes you fifty years to finally get it – your life as it is intended - "right" then so be it. Now, you may arrive to the point of actualization in one piece or maybe even broken, confused, bruised and exhausted. Either way you will arrive. It all depends on what you do, believe and follow NOW.

This is all the more reason why deliberating the truth of who you really are is crucial. When you do this, you will start to see that the time it takes for a thought to become a reality gets shorter and shorter.

Now let's talk about how determining whether or not you are choosing what is "wrong" for you by following other people's "rights". As I stated previously, we can sometimes look at how the events of our lives unfold to help us determine whether or not we have made a habit out of living in accordance to what is right in the eyes of others. It may be best to start off with asking yourself a few key questions that will give you a better understanding of that which you are verses that which you are not:

1. Who am I at the core of my being?
2. What is my purpose, my truth or my message?
3. Is fulfilling a purpose and carrying out my mission even necessary or am I alright with simply existing until it is time for me to transcend physical form?

I encourage you to really take the time to listen for your true answers. It is unwise to settle for the first few answers that come to mind. I recommend putting this book down for a few minutes, few hours or even a few days before continuing. Hearing the correct answers to these queries is what will help you make the first fundamental steps toward living in accordance to your truth. May I also suggest writing down your answers, especially to question number one.

Here is a tip: when answering "Who am I at the core of my being?" try to think beyond the moment. Tap into remembrance of the person you prophesied being when you were a child. Consider your gifts, your talent and your unique abilities that have been lying dormant consequent to the negative words and opinions offered by your elders. Rekindle your relationship with the envisioned being that you have suppressed as a result of fear. Also, allow yourself take wonder in the legacy you feel compelled to leave behind once your lifetime here on earth has reached its end. Think of all your natural characteristics, your innate desires, your hopes and your dreams…think of all of the things that radiates from the authentic self, things or experiences

216

that if carried out would make you the most joyous, centered, fulfilled and humble yet proud person on this planet.

Now, that you have your answers, here is where the most pivotal conversation with yourself must occur. Here is where you begin to compare what you are doing or how you are living and behaving NOW to the life you know to be true in your heart and mind; the life you know you are meant to live from the depths of your soul.

Remember I mentioned the concept of using your feelings as an emotional compass to gauge how close you are to self-actualization, or even how far off course you may be to living from your authentic vision? Since you have taken the first commendable step to deeply connecting with the truth of your original self, be encouraged to ponder answers to the following questions:

1. How do I feel about the state of my existence in this very moment?

2. How do I hope to feel as I get back into alignment?

3. Who am I and what am I doing when no one else is looking that attributes or detracts from the life I aspire to live and the goals I aspire to reach?

4. Am I living the truth of my authentic/spirited self?

5. How close am I to living my truth, and what is it that I need to bring me closer to the self I envision?

Answers to these questions will also be useful in your endeavor to live life fully and in complete awareness of your choices and decisions. Most importantly, they will help you discern whether or not you are living in accordance to what others (family, friends, spouses, parents etc.) may think best for your life.

Do not be alarmed if and when you discover that you have not been living your authentic life. This would entail an attitude of judgment that is harmful and violent towards your soul. The truth of the matter is that the majority of people in this world are too afraid to live from the inside out. It takes a certain amount of courage and healthy rebellion to stand up and live in truth to what it is you feel in your Spirit, as well as, in harmony with the your unique gifts, talents and passions, despite what others may think of you. It takes a certain amount of strength and maturity to decipher and comprehend implications that are impressed on your mind if and when you feel either on course or out of alignment with your purpose.

As an individual who is obviously ready to overcome the buts and start living your truth, I challenge you to dig a litter deeper and contemplate how you would feel if your time on earth reached its end and you I never lived your truth. There have been countless cases where successful people experience tearful transitions simply because they died with their "song still inside of them." I imagine there is no amount of money that could quiet the regret one fills for having spent their time being and living by someone else's standards, rules, concepts and beliefs.

As you move into your next level of awareness, make certain that you fully understand the importance of being attuned to your emotions. From this instant forward, be aware of how useful your feelings are in your endeavor to reach goals and dreams. Good emotions (happy, inspired, enthusiastic, loved, courageous, strong, peaceful, elated, encouraged or blissful) indicate that you are on course and in alignment with your truth. And of course, negative emotions (anxiety, frustration, disappointment, anger, rejection, sadness, fear, and resentment) reveal opportunities for healing or improvement – inward and outward – that involve making better choices. It is through reflection that you will be enabled to discover what sacrificial decisions and modifications must be rendered in order to stay on the constant path of reaching for what feels better, moment-by-moment.

Here are a few more queries that will get you moving toward living your truth and away from the habit of cowering to the conditions and expectations that others have on your life.

1. Am I at peace with where I am today?
2. How would I like to feel?
3. What do I need to do to get me on track to feeling better about my life in this moment? (start small so that these goals are attainable and not too overwhelming)

Though no one can accomplish their dreams or become the person they envision overnight. The overall goal or vision can sometimes be overwhelming, which inadvertently causes inertia. Thus, neither right nor wrong choices can be made, which essentially makes it very difficult to move from one level of potential to the next. If this is the case for you, simply take the time to ponder all of the questions in this chapter. Digest all of your thoughts and emotions and simply allow them to be. Listen for the small voice inside your head before you make a move. If still the thoughts are too overpowering, start by asking this one question: What would make me feel most comfortable to have completed by the end of this day? When you can move from day to week, to month to year, you will discover that you are well on your way to creating the life to which you aspire.

It only takes a blink for you to recognize the essence of that which is truly you. Rather than a blink, this time, close your eyes for a moment longer and introduce yourself to greatness. Take a few seconds to breathe in the elements of life that share the same essentials from which you are also created. Delve deeper within and trust on the power of your mind. Remind yourself that everything you need exists within you. Honor the connection between you, relationships, resources that are showing up right now to help you manifest your dreams and live your life the "right" way. Appreciate the harmonious reunion as you confidently and boldly become reacquainted with You. Cherish the moment, as you become one who endeavors to bring your personal and spiritual minds into alignment so that you may focus energy on right thoughts, right actions and right responses to create the life that is right for you. Smile and lovingly embrace yourself, an individual who is now fearless, successful, strong and resilient. Now call forth an image of your imagined self. Envision the collaboration that takes place as the two of you merge to become one with truth and embark upon a real journey that was once a dream.

"Not what we have but what we enjoy, constitutes our abundance."

- Epicurus

Claiming Your Inheritance

Inheritance.

If you look up the word inheritance in the dictionary, you may find it defined as the genetic traits transmitted from parent to offspring or something received from predecessors by or as if by succession. It may even be described as a passing of property upon the owner's death to the heir or those entitled to succeed. Now, when asked to define inheritance off the top of our heads, most of us would refer to it as our legacy, birthright, or heritage or a large sum of money left behind by a deceased relative. Moving beyond the material, one thing we neglect to perceive as something inherited is our sense of being. Unfortunately, it takes many of us a lifetime (or even a few, depending on one's beliefs and level of awareness) to figure out how applying the principle of inheritance to our individual and collective existences can enhance or create an entirely different actuality. It can potentially raise our level of responsibility or bring clarity to the standpoint through which we perceive and live our lives.

Should we choose to recognize that the life and body in which we each currently exist is indeed one of which was inherited the day we came into this world, we just may begin to attract different experiences, people and circumstances; ones that contribute to or are in alignment with the overall intention for our journey. This would, of course, entail being deliberately conscious of our life intention or purpose. Regardless of our position or level of understanding, we can all agree by now that we are not here by accident. We are meant to be HERE, in this present moment, as a result of both our divine and biological annuity. Whether we believe it was received by way of our parents, grandparents and ancestors, or through an expanded awareness of creation which moves us into the comprehension that we are simply "the small of what the Creator is in the large", the bottom line is this: none of us appeared on this Earth without cause. Therefore, the breath we breathe, the blood running through our veins, muscles and tissue, the mind we develop, and the energy that fuels our spirit, and the heart through which we feel was not shaped through some form of spontaneous magic.

Everything we experience, realize, and recognize is possible consequent to the life made physically present to us at birth, including the mind that determines the perception of our realities. Everyone was born with the birthright or entitlement to succeed, expand, learn and thrive to the best of our abilities. For whatever reason, there are some of us who are able to cash in on these provisions; then there are others who remain lax in allowing their opportunities to burgeon pass them by. Living life with the highest intention to fulfill the unspoken promise that comes when we accept our divine inheritance is the key to achieving harmony and prosperity. It's what helps us transcend excuses and justifications for living small. Simply put: any encounters with wealth or good health and well-being, or any bouts we have with poverty and disease occurs contingent upon the level of connection maintained and aligned with our entitlement to succeed, prosper and flourish.

Upon further speculation, who do you know that has taken well to something of which was gifted, but was in poor condition upon receipt. Though this may initially sound self-centered, but realistically, how likely is it for anyone to be ecstatic over an insignificant endowment, menial, undervalued, something more of a hindrance than it is a contribution to one's level of influence, affluence or achievement? On the other side of the coin, we hear stories told everyday of one's appreciation, excitement and elation when they discovered that they were the recipients of something substantial and momentous. It is in the moment we begin to look at our own lives – mind, body and soul – in this same capacity that we will begin to witness a shift in our own lives and how it occurs to and for us. As long as we continue to perceive this existence as something to struggle through, bear, or carry out, there will always be a void, a sense of lack and discontent. It is to the degree in which we are willing to pay attention, using time and energy as our means of exchange, that we will experience what occurs in the world around us. If we expect pain or lack, we will experience things painfully, disdainfully, doubtfully and fearfully. This hinders progress and evolution. If we expect to experience increase, success and fulfillment, we will experience things lovingly, excitedly, and abundantly. This, of course, promotes the freedom for expansion, increase and fulfillment.

Imagine that someone told you at birth that your life was valued at $5,000,000, but only if you shared your gifts, talents, and innate state of being (peace, joy, unconditional love and servitude), while simultaneously striving to reach your highest potential. I guarantee you, your whole outlook would change to one filled with anticipation, exhilaration, value and self-worth.

Your faith and trust in our ability to succeed would be tremendously heightened and uninhibited.

Instead of seeing our worth, as well as, the opportunity to create a legacy through our inheritance, most of us make the mistake of being disgruntled about our current circumstances and situations; we take to complaining and competing, discounting and distrusting what we envision instead of living in the radiance of our gifts. And when others appear to be living the lives we'd prefer, we grow consumed with envy and succumb to the urge to conform as a means of acquiring what we desire. Instead of reflecting or "seeing the silver lining" beyond what is, we sometimes disprove everything we ever believed or learned. We lose sight of our deep-rooted objectives while stumbling blindly in the darkness beneath our "burdens." We grow overwhelmed under the weight of disappointment; we misplace the confidence we need to surmount obstacles and challenges. In doing so, we allow sentiments of defeat to discourage us from staying the course of the intended outcome of our journey, despite what our environments and circumstances may suggest. Thus, we block the flow of our own inheritance by living in fear, lack of focus, in-authenticity, or by catering to distractions that do not fall in line with our truest aspirations.

Consider that maybe "intention is not just something you do, but rather a force that exists in the universe as an invisible field of energy from which we are privileged to call forth visions and the steps that coincide with fruition. If this is the case, it is quite possible that we have made our lives and the duty of working diligently for what we want a little more difficult than necessary. It suggests that we consider the option of simply envisioning our lives as we prefer, staying in alignment with our true inheritance, listening to and trusting our inner authority, tapping into the field of intention and power, creating, loving and living with purpose and allowing all that we aspire for our lives to crystallize on its own accordance. We could do away with forcefully striving to achieve through manipulation, following other people's formulas for success, or strategically positioning ourselves to be in the right place at the right time. Maybe intention has very thing to do with living up to our inheritance, to leave behind a legacy that withstands time. Is it possible that our natural inheritance was never something to be sought, but rather allowed and invited to exist in our lives by simply being it?

Aligning your mind, spirit and body for the effective and conscious creation of your preferred experiences doesn't mean things will harmoniously change overnight. Trust that it takes diligence and practice. It takes focus and strength. It takes courage to move away from the ego and remaining firmly planted within your power, love, faith and integrity. It involves living from your spirit, your heart space where you can feel whether or not you we on the right path. Below is a list of actions to be practiced in order to increase the level of fulfillment, to live up to our fullest potential, and to be a worthy recipient of this precious gift we call life.

Remember, these are things that can be exercised NO MATTER WHAT may be occurring around you. The more you practice, the less unreasonable these theories appear, and the easier it gets to implement them into your daily thoughts, actions and overall existence. Claiming our inheritance and living up to your legacy entails:

- Pointing attention in the right direction
- Centering energies on all that is positive and loving
- Managing thoughts and emotions (doing away with negativities and fears)
- Releasing resentment and administering random acts of kindness (despite circumstances…)
- Living in the space of gratitude

- Staying complete, transparent, vulnerable, available and open to yourself, as well as others
- Widening your awareness
- Expanding your sense of creativity and using talents and gifts in service of others
- Communing with nature; appreciating life
- Casting nets in the "right" bodies of water
- Flocking together with like-minded individuals
- Raising the bar of your environments and associates (avoid being the smartest person you know)
- Connecting with everything inspiring
- Speaking goodness about life and expressing your truth
- Rehabilitating self-esteem and remaining humble on the threshold of success
- Tapping into the source of infinite wisdom, love, peace, and intelligence
- Paying attention with the right forms of exchange
- Bringing completion to everything you start

These are some things that can be attributed to healing relationships, finding new ways to create revenue, losing weight, releasing pain form past experiences, pursuing new careers and undying passions, starting a business or anything else that has been lying dormant at the core of your heart. In the event that you could use a little more help with getting from point A to point B, to bring your dreams and aspirations to reality, invest the time and energy into attaining a trainer, attend seminars and workshops, or even build a library of books penned for enrichment and elevation.

By now, most of us should be aware that the life (all of which encompasses the collective of moments we call past, present and future) we have been given the opportunity to live, is actually a gift that we inherited the day we were born. In the event that you have yet to come to this realization, it is highly suggested that you make a slight yet significant shift in your perspective. This way, you not only increase your level of awareness of why and what is or is not occurring in your world, but you grow more enabled to take advantage of your chance to prosper as the creator of each and every experience you encounter.

Inspirational writer Ricky Roberts III says, "Life is a gift that gives your soul a place to be." Sometimes, such a dynamic outlook can be a bit overwhelming to us. The vast array of possibility that is available between our birth and death, our beginning and moment of transcendence, can have us stumbling in confusion without any sense of direction. Thus, it is easily to be distracted by our own selfish intentions, delusions, or for some of us, a sense of grandeur. We lose sight of the authentic self that gets buried beneath the mountain of "buts" we use to justify our sense of incompletion or failure, and gives reason for the trail of missed opportunities lingering behind us.

"Champions have the courage to keep turning the pages because they know a better chapter lies ahead."

- Pastor Paula White

Your Promotion

Sometimes rising above temporary circumstances (pleasant or otherwise) or stagnation occurs when we simply take the time to review and reflect on the perspectives and perceptions we hold about who, what and where we are in our lives. It involves stepping back and reshaping our minds (the cause), which can change our environments (the conditions) in a way that warrant our ability to align ourselves with greater results (effects). The majority of us have a great yearning to answer a "calling", to behave boldly or adhere to the willingness to be worthy. There is an impulse we have within that compels us respond to the urge to find adventure in our adversity. Yet, more often than not, we find great challenge in discovering ways to go about reaching such an accomplishment.

Truthfully, the road to overcoming this challenge not only lies in how we perceive our lives, but also in how we go about participating in it. Some of us are highly mistaken by the notion that merely existing or observing the coming and goings of people and circumstances amounts to "living". When what this really implies is an inclination to allow life to pass them by. If we are not contributing to or actively participating in our existences, we deny our souls and the Source the very platform it needs to experience itself through us, by us, as us, and most importantly for us.

Now, if the "soul's desire" perspective of what is possible between the present moment and the remainder of your physical life is off-putting, let's consider some other alternatives to maintaining a perspective that empowers you to reach your preferred experience of actualization. In a practical sense, it is quite possible that up until this point you have been managing your life as a project that is made up of a series of smaller projects. Some of which have been completed, others remain incomplete, while the majority can be found lingering between the spaces of imagination and fruition.

Allow me to use the metaphor of maintaining a job (an acronym for just over broke) as it relates to holding the position of Project Manager. With this in mind, realize that as "project manager" you are still reliant upon individuals to dictate when you have or have not successfully reached a certain goal and how you should be compensated. Though the job is great and possibly even lucrative, there are still a set of reins that bind you from making decisions without the contingency of approval by a higher power. All of your resources, staff, tools, space, time and equipment to ensure success and completion are provided consequent to the availability of someone else's budget. One of the greatest skills that you can accrue as a project manager is the ability to adjust, adapt and execute. Otherwise, you would be out of a job. However immense your list of responsibilities and compensation, you are still only a manager; not the person in charge.

Now, let's slightly shift your perspective. What do you think would happen if you were to perceive yourself and position in life as being on the brink of a promotion? What if you started to take on an attitude of liability, rather than that of a worker-bee, follower or people pleaser? True, you have worked hard up until this point and have grown comfortable with the sense of security (the safety of monotony and never taking risks) you have built. But when will you be ready to take the reins and the reign over the legacy you aspire to leave behind once your time here on Earth has reached its end. What would life look like if you were empowered by the greatness you have inherited? Even though the "how" may be a little unclear, consider what would be available to you if you took a risk; if you surrendered the controlling need to know how your vision will transpire; if actually took the courageous step that moves you beyond the threshold separating you from the present state of existence to your preferred state of existence; if you understood how the subtle difference between working towards your destiny and living your destiny largely effects your ability to let go of hindering excuses.

Something that you inherited the day you were born is the constant gift of promotion. Today, you are being promoted to CEO of the company called Your Life.

Up until now, you have been managing this company, and now you have the authority of running it in alliance with the Owner, Source, or Higher Power. In your position as the Creative Expression of Oneness, it is your duty to ensure unification (mind, body and spirit; self, Self and Source; you, your community and the universe, etc.) through the utilization of your gifts, skills, talents and ultimately your purpose.

Like any other successful company, a mission and vision must be followed to guarantee longevity, universal contribution, outstanding service and profit that allows you to sustain the livelihood of those whom uphold your vision – including you. Your mission is to take advantage of every opportunity and possibility you can to convey as much divine love, peace, power, wellness, compassion and abundance in all that you do, create, say and speak. Your vision is to inspire others to do the same through the unique products and services your company provides. As enlivening as this endeavor may feel, the overall intention is to remain humble in your position, stay open to expansion and continue maintaining and honoring those who support and patronize your company.

One cannot grow successful without ever making mistakes or failures. I once heard that "the only risk in failure is promotion," Our responsibility as CEO of our companies is to make certain that we flourish and thrive beyond let downs and disappointment by making proper alliances, minimizing deficiencies and rising above the illusion of defeat. Knowledge and wisdom are to be woven into the fibers of our infrastructure so that our business continues to grow, produce and profit in ways that allow us to become philanthropists of happiness and goodness. Your Life is merely an outwardly expressions of your overall purpose and intention for success and fulfillment, no matter how miniscule or grand.

Congratulations on your promotion!!! Celebrate the wonderful opportunities for confronting your fears, manifesting your dreams and creating the success you've always imagined.

Reminder: As CEO - Creative Expression of Oneness – of a company called Your Life, your mission is to take advantage of every opportunity and possibility you can to convey as much divine love, peace, power, wellness, compassion and abundance in all that you do, say and speak. Your vision is to inspire others to do the same through the unique products and services your company provides. Always cultivate prosperity and profit for the sake of being a philanthropist of happiness and service beyond the self.

"Perception is a mirror not a fact. And what I look on is my state of mind, reflected outward."

\-   A Course in Miracles

Perceptions

Have you ever considered the misconception regarding the adage "perception is reality"? Looking closely, you will find that the fallacy revolves around the word "is", which ultimately implies exactness, factuality and accuracy. Truthfully, the perceptions in which we indulge are used to create the realities we perceive to be authentic and unwavering. Perception – an attitude or understanding based on what is observed or thought – is what we use to help shape and formulate judgments, beliefs and opinions about the things and people that come in and out of our lives.

Example: 'I would love to write a book, but I can't because..."

The statement above indicates that the speaker has succumbed to the false perception of being unable or incapable of fulfilling a desire. As the co-creator of her life inability is never true. There is always a way. The opposing perception written above is only "made true" to the speaker through the "but" that stands in the gap between the vision and the justification. Keep in mind, the only real relationship she is ever having is with herself. This means that no matter what comes after because, she is the only person in this equation accountable for creating a reason not to fulfill her desire. The same would apply if she were to speak about different, more constructive reality.

As mentioned in previous chapters, the limitations we ponder are always created in the mind over which we have authority. If ever we choose to stop thinking, the problem of not being able to complete a goal or reach an aspiration would dissolve. Instead of worrying or trying to figure out the how, we could very well place the same energy into creating a possibility that is in compliance with All That Is Good.

Checking to make sure our perceptions are accurate and worthy of holding can be done by asking one simple question: Is that true? Again, what becomes true for us is based on the perspectives and perceptions we hold in our minds. There is great power in comprehending Law of Mind in Action which implies that nothing can exist or be experienced that did not first exist in thought form.

When mindful, we can also begin to see how false perceptions become the very elements that perpetuate the vivacity of our outlook. This impacts the way we experience people, situations, circumstances and environments. Going one step further, we can also witness how many of our perceptions transpire contingent upon what we aspire or avoid.

More likely than not, we base our entire state of existence on the perceptions we've obtained throughout our lives. Our ego has a large part to play in this, being that it filters temporary or transitory observances, all external to the self, in a fashion that resonates according to where we happen to be in our life at any particular moment. Often times our perceptions are shaped around concepts and sensations that were either passed down from others or came into our awareness as a result encountering and/or enduring circumstances that have impacted our sense of being – negatively or positively. Seldom are we mindful enough to deal with, comprehend or stay attuned to the reality of what is taking place in the current moment without relying on the thoughts, ideas and memories accrued throughout our journey. Here is where error rears its head: Not always are our perceptions true and authentic in a capacity that allows us to know and experience ourselves as freely as intended for our life.

For that reason, we must begin to understand how we have/are creating our lives based solely on one out of several aspects of how things occur. How can anyone perceive anything to be entirely true without the complete story? Better explained, how can anything be an "is" without all of the elements that make "it" so, or not so?

Example: Staying focused on the road ahead while driving does not ensure the safety of those in and/or outside of your vehicle. The full perspective is necessary if and when you decide to switch lanes, speed up or slow down. You must be able to observe from all angles when obstacles impede your pace or obstruct your view. The smoothness, speed and synchronicity of your fellow drivers may present the semblance that all is well, but it isn't until you get the full representation of what "is" that you will be able to navigate effectively. Once you are capable of observing the entire scope of traffic – including vehicles hidden within your blind spots - through your rear and side view mirrors, you then become more empowered to reach your destination without harming yourself and others. The same should apply to the courses in which we pursue or endeavor to reach our goals and objectives throughout our daily interactions.

So in actuality, perception is not reality; perception generates reality illusions that help us to cope in our existence. There is actually nothing wrong with envisioning outcomes and results based on what we see and observe. It is merely one mental function of our human being-ness. But imagine how much more effective we could be in producing possibilities, or making choices and decisions, based on one of three things: tapping into an awareness and assessing situations in totality; opening the mind in such a way that allows us to see beyond appearance, sound and emotion; and/or letting go of our perceptions so that we may deal with what is and not the stories that make up what we identify as "right" or "true."

In essence, evolution has found us at a point where we have become the habit of coloring our existence with emotions roused through incomplete ideas and understandings to formulate thoughts, beliefs and judgments about how things appear. We breathe validity into our perceptions through the stories and justifications that enable us to manage our lives as painlessly as possible; or, as agonizingly as possible, for those who tend to perpetuate victimization. Therefore, our belief in the stories about what we perceive to be true actually keeps us from realizing the truth of our journey or existence. Why, because most of what we perceive is rooted in fear; or quite possibly founded on the premise that avoiding the things we dread keeps us safe from harm, guilt, destruction and discomfort. Therefore, perceptions come in handy in our need to pacify the impact of occurrences that do not coincide with our idea of security and welfare. Interestingly enough, the necessity to evade distress actually prevents us from taking heed and experiencing "what is really true in this now moment" of our lives in fullness. Reason being is that we are more likely to react to situations that arise, or to the perception of how the situation seems to be unfolding, rather than being, living freely and openly; taking it all in, so to speak, without judgment. Keep in mind, free in this context does not mean being unbound by entities that threaten oppression (thoughts, opinions, circumstances and behaviors of others); but more so, in our ability to allow the spirit within to flourish in every area of our lives without hindrance.

Having or holding any perception at all implies that other possibilities or viewpoints exist; one or some of which we rather not give attention in order to maintain our "rightful" position.

Take a moment to ponder the full meaning of that last statement.

The fact that you have a perception at all means that there are still other aspects about a particular subject, condition or individual to know and/or acquire in order for you to be certain of its presence. All of this is crucial in becoming aware of the relativity between you and your relationships, journey, purpose, passion mission, or even your excuses. However, deciphering what really is from your perception or filtered observations can arouse perplexity as one sojourns toward the realization of complete self-expression. A great starting point to aid in your ability to distinguish between the true and untrue in the matter of self-actualization comes with comprehending what true perception comprises: all authentic perceptions are derivative of viewing occurrences (your life) from a vantage point founded on love, not fear.

Now keep in mind, holding anything outside of a true perception about an occurrence means that you have granted meaning to something to validate your sense of identity and existence, which in turn gives you some-thing for which to compete, fight and stand. This being the case, it is imperative that you begin to understand just how much maintaining an inadvertent position of rivalry and opposition distracts you from engaging in the gift of being. Focusing on obscurity –only one aspect of appearance - disallows all that exists around you to be and be experienced exactly as IT is.

To minimize confusion, it would help to transfer your energies towards getting to a place of knowing, rather than perceiving. This is a concept that may only be mid-wifed through a strong sense of being; it entails studying yourself; it involves being in complete oneness with your mind, body and especially the soul/spirit/self. The whole reason for our presence here on Earth is so that we may express, create and know ourselves outwardly and limitlessly. We become successful in this endeavor the moment we begin to reduce the amount of energy we disburse toward our opinions, our thoughts, and our perceptions. We can opt to expand, explore and master the art of possibility, attraction, participation and the cultivation of insight and awareness beyond temporary and physical evidence.

There is no such thing as death where life is being lived; there is no such thing as life where amidst the experience of death. One can only precede or follow the other, but they cannot be both experienced at the same time. Yet we as humans tend to balance the existence of both by living in fear of one, while capitalizing the existence of the other. In this case, most of us fear death, yet we do our best to make the most of everything we think encompasses life. Our perceptions give definition to our lives or our environments that prohibit, as well as, enhance our awareness; focusing attention on both facets creates conflict in our commitment to reach self-actualization.

We cannot be both committed to avoiding fear and flourishing in love. It is simpler, and much more conducive to the unfolding of our divinity to choose one state of being and focusing all of our attention upon it. The same is applicable with harm vs. harmony, danger vs. peace, light vs. darkness, joy vs. pain, etc. One cannot exist in the company of the other. Darkness cannot thrive in the presence of light. If you are "light" you grow more empowered when you live as our radiance and nothing else, regardless of your surrounding; understanding there is such a thing as darkness is much different than holding on to your perception of and being darkness.

How would your life would unfold if you simply – and it is quite simple – chose to be life rather than contemplating the concept of death, which inevitably provokes fear. Listening to the resounding "yes" of the universe, will also help in doing away with false perceptions and point you toward perceptions and "inlooks" that are true. You become equipped to consciously arrive to each moment of your life whole and complete. Totality can never be fulfilled living life through perception; only through living in truth. Living your life for and from your inner-being consummates living a highly valued life of contribution, accountability, forgiveness and freedom.

As spiritual beings having a human experience, we have the power choose how we evolve and how we intend to experience our life. We have the opportunity to know and proceed accordingly in our life experience, rather than perceive and avoid what may or may not be occurring. Being able to choose, know and live our lives in truth empowers us make the primary decision to be fully present, joyous, loving, harmonious, whole, prosperous, and abundant in our giving. Thus, we remain cognizant of the notion to be or choosing something out of alignment with divine decision means we have decided "wrongly".

More from the Tao te Ching:
When people see some things as beautiful,
other things become ugly.
When people see some things as good,
other things become bad.

Practice not-doing,
and everything will fall into place.

When you are content to be simply yourself
and don't compare or compete,
everybody will respect you.

Giving birth and nourishing,
having without possessing,
acting with no expectations,
leading and not trying to control:
this is the supreme virtue.

We are not our bodies or our circumstances. These are merely physical devices used by the ego to remind us of the differences and distinctions that prevent us from connecting with and to one another. By focusing on the power of Love-Light-Life

244

encapsulated within, we can begin to approach situations in an assured, amorous state of being rather than avoid circumstances on account of our fear of being extinguished or unrecognized.

Because your radiance is so infectious, begin to be accountable for ceasing the perpetuation of fear. Refrain from conspiring with others about all the things that went wrong in previous encounters and experiences. Instead of warning or listing all the caveats of potential outcomes that others may experiences as a result of your own fears, pain and discomfort, focus on and teach the good, the wisdom, the knowledge and the evolution that you have attained consequent to overcoming your challenges. Intelligence of mind gives you the ability to choose how you live. Being a loving demonstration of power and perseverance inevitably tutors others in the process of simply being what they believe to be true for themselves.

Another habit which we have a tendency to partake is maintaining the perception that we are always being attacked by another's presence, thoughts, ideas, and perspectives. When one does not fall in line or agree with our perceptions, beliefs and mindsets, the first inclination we follow is the need to defend. Therefore, the place from which we live, observe and listen is founded on judgments, opinions, and illusions that have already been formulated from past experiences.

To feel attacked by anything is to deny that you are "okay" in all of your actions, planning, thinking and being. However, to deny anything is to at least recognize that it exists or existed; to recognize that it exists means that you had to have somewhere along the way experienced whatever you are denying. It is impossible to deny something you have never experienced – even if such experience came by way of witnessing someone else's failure. Whatever the case may be, it is most likely that you experienced what you are now denying and perceiving in the form of dislike. This causes you to disown what was once a part of your being, and ultimately putting off onto others exactly how

245

and what you perceive to be disdainful. This form of discernment disallows you to connect with others who disagree with your sense of being, which prohibits you from experiencing anything outside of your own awareness.

As you can see, our need to hold fast to and/or maintain our perceptions (all of which we believe to be true) completely limits our potential for having peace, productivity, progress and prosperity in our lives. The possibilities that can transpire the moment you shift from living from the place of defense or denial to a place of appreciation and acceptance are endless. This is so because your whole experience of the world and those you encounter changes from conflict and fear to an exchange of love and meaning. You lose the desire to be "right" and become more open in your awareness in a way that enables experiences to be just as they are. Life begins to evolve from lack and worry that comes when living in denial to one of abundance and gratitude.

Just as much as fear is a reality, so is its opposite. It is your job to learn to let go of your fears, so that you may create the space to live a life that is enlivened, inspiring and fulfilling. Do this by nurturing your intentions with courage, compassion, truth, optimism and love. Otherwise, you will suffocate the dreams and desires of your heart before they even had a chance to break soil. There is a Taoism quote that reads: "Be careful what you water your dreams with. Water them with worry and fear and you will produce weeds that choke the life from your dream. Water them with optimism and solutions and you will cultivate success. Always be on the lookout for ways to turn a problem into an opportunity for success. Always be on the lookout for ways to nurture your dream."

So again, perception is not reality until we make it so. The perceptions we harbor construct our realities. The aptitude of creation makes us entirely responsible for how reality occurs to and for us. By stepping back and gaining a broader perspective of "what really is", we empower ourselves to create more desired realities. Essentially, we then become the circumstances and experiences that resonate with our well-being rather than perceive them.

It is not your responsibility to make your previous experience manifest in the lives of others. Making the decision to be compassionately optimistic in your sharing allows you to inspire and encourage others to look for avenues of love and creativity, rather than running from something that has yet to occur. Thus, fear can be extinguished with the fostering of bravery, affection and wisdom.

"By helping others achieve their dreams, you will achieve yours."

– Les Brown

Kindness in the Journey to Success

*O*ne key to success or fulfillment is to refrain ourselves from entertaining selfish intentions. Being selfless frees up space, time and energy to help others create success for themselves. Being mindful of how we use our gifts, skills and talents to be charitable and compassionate acts as an investment towards what will harvest as a blessing in other areas of your life.

The more we focus on being of service and helping others flourish, the more effective or fruitful we become in our own lives. We can each start the process of achievement or fulfillment by displaying random acts of kindness.

I challenge you to practice offering random acts of kindness for five days straight. I have provided some tips to help you complete this intention for the week.

Day One:

Pay Attention, Listen and Be Present

Set the intention to release inner-conversation about self-centered, self-seeking and self-serving opportunities, perspectives, objectives, judgments and the desire to conspire or relate with one's experiences while they are talking. Allow yourself to focus on another person's, especially someone whom may be encountering upset, discontent or discomfort similar to what you are or have already experienced. Instead of absentmindedly offering your opinion or advice, inquire about what exactly you can do for them, but only when they are done expressing themselves. Actively participate in their attempt to gain acceptance, understanding, comfort or resolution.

Day Two:

Make an Introduction (offer a list of resources or share

your professional and social network)

Move beyond the apprehension that keeps you from exchanging information and opportunities that will enable someone else to prosper. Do away with the diseased mindset that compels you to hoard your talents, gifts and resources consequent to your fear of someone else succeeding before you. Understand that stockpiling resources implies the perception that fortuity would be stunted or forfeited in your attempt to help another. This is the fear of lack speaking. Where is love in all of this? You never know what chance for advancement you may be passing up in your unwillingness to share knowledge, wealth, contacts and connections. Make another choice.

Day Three:

Support Someone Else's Dream (offer your services or

product for free)

Success is breathing life into other people and their dreams as a result of you living and pursuing your own passion and purpose. But this doesn't mean staying blind to the fact that you can be more than an inspiration. We aren't always cognizant of our tendency to cache resources, talents and gifts as we go about our day-to-day lives working, raising families, and creating ways to sustain a sense of completion and fulfillment in our own lives. When further considered, how does staying tunnel-minded contribute to any form of prosperity, maturation or profit? There are also times where we feel compelled to give yet the concept of lack keeps us from recognizing opportunities for bestowment that dwells in the womb of creativity. Philanthropy doesn't always have to manifest in a monetary fashion. You can help another along their journey to destiny by being supportive, granting your time to handle small administrative tasks, offering a listening ear, developing an idea, keeping their aspirations in high, sharing loving thoughts, exercising patience, etc.

Sometimes it is the small things that people do that make us feel large, brilliant, worthy, gifted and strong enough to go beyond limits in pursuit of their dreams. Be an inspiration today, by doing something small that can go a really long way.

Day Four:

Pay Forward an Act of Kindness Someone Offered You

None of us got where we are in our lives by sheer luck or happenstance. Honor this by paying forward an act of kindness or service. The objective is to keep your intention pure as you follow through with intention Any action you take should be done with a selfless spirit, or borne from the space of gratitude for all of the countless deeds from others we have encountered along our journey.

Lovingly choose to be the cornerstone to someone else's benefit without expectation or compensation. The easiest way to do this is to carry out an action or offer a gift to a person or group of people anonymously. This doesn't have to be large gesture, but should be executed from the abundant place in your heart that yearns to help others, make a difference or simply bring a smile to frowning face.

Day Five:

Apologize, Forgive and Release Pain (for both you and anyone involved)

There is healing in forgiveness. When the action of another arouses pain, rather than instinctively reacting, be hasty in your movement towards forgiveness. True, it may be difficult to hold light to someone who has brought discomfort to your wellbeing, especially as a result of selfish intentions. Understand you do not have to do this alone. Sometimes it starts with inviting Spirit into your heart and allowing the love you have for self and the Creator to carry you on your river of mercy where healing flows. The sooner this is done, the sooner you can get back to the joyous life you deserve

When we give to others or contribute to one's growth and evolution, we cancel out negative energy, thoughts and emotions we may be experiencing in our current circumstances. This ultimately which frees up space in our hearts, minds and environments for the sharing of creative ideas, resources, good deeds, referrals, assistance, etc.

Afterthought

*T*here are several things that occur throughout our lives that move us in and out of certain stages of our evolution as human beings. Some are painful; some are enlightening; and some generate moments filled with joy, while others may foster a spiritual awakening that can never be forgotten. There are very few, however, that encompass all four of the elements I just listed. I can say today, that I am fortunate to have had one of these types of experiences. As much as it pains me to share this occurrence with you, it is my intent to show how life-altering experiences can be used to move mountains in your pathway leading to success, fulfillment or happines.

I recently lost a very close friend of mine who was diagnosed with a life-threatening disease only nine months prior to her passing. It was as her health began rapidly deteriorating that I felt inclined to pen the pages of this book. I will be truthful in saying that watching her go from a healthy, independent and vibrant individual to a frail, reliant and lifeless being tore my heart into a million pieces. However, as incredibly difficult as this period of my own life may have been, I could never clear my heart of the empathy I held for her demise. How dare I consider my pain? Wasn't she the one suffering? I ached terribly, however there was no way I could be so selfish. It wasn't easy, but setting aside my own self-regarding feelings so that I could hold her hand through the different stages of her illness was comforting to both of us. The thought of her suffering through this phase in her life without me by her side was not something I could have lived with it. The comprehension that her life would soon come to an end is what kept me in the front row, applauding and encouraging the best performance in the final act of her years on earth. And though I hated to see her suffer, I am so very grateful for the time we spent together – even up to the day she passed away.

In the end, the truth of the matter is that her nine-month battle was the most exhausting, sorrowful and most arduous occurrence I'd ever endured in all of my thirty-six years.

As to be expected, memories of those days are both filled with agony and joy, especially now that she is "gone." However, it is not her passing that saddens me most when it comes to accepting her physical absence. The lessons I learned about life at the expense of hers came through watching how she conducted herself throughout this trial. In part, it was a beautiful sight to see how much she was loved, as friends from all over the country put forth great effort into "letting her see her flowers" before her time came to an end. As a loving mother, daughter, sister and wife, she'd managed to unknowingly impact hundreds of people's lives, just by being herself – funny, vivacious, caring, and loving. Words cannot express the gratitude I feel in knowing that God allowed her to see just how much she meant to people before she said goodbye.

There is another side to this story that I must share with the sole purpose of portraying the full gist of why and how much this encounter has affected me. It is the hidden force that pushed me to inscribe this powerful message so that others may also be inspired to make appropriate, healthy and constructive choices and decisions. I feel compelled to state first and foremost that the following memories are not the only ones I have of my Dear Sister in Spirit. There are many that are extremely influential and enlightening. We shared many great times filled with fun and laughter and all the ups and downs that best friends bear together. Needless to say, my reminiscences of our friendship will be treasured forever. I am merely using the accounts that I am about to disclose as an example of how and why we as women should choose to live the greatest lives our imaginations can conceive. And we should choose to live them NOW. I am certain the sharing of this account will encourage you in the same way that it consistently restores my faith whenever I am reminded. Because I know that millions of women around the world stay in situations that may be unhealthy, I offer these words with intentions to enthuse…not to place judgment.

Though I wish this were not the case, what most people did not know about my friend was that well beneath the façade that "everything was fine in her world," lived an extremely unhappy and lonely person. Sure, she had her children, loving sisters, bothers and mother; she had the nice house in the suburb with two cars parked in the driveway and a lucrative job at a prominent Fortune 500 company. Underneath her loving exterior

255

was a woman who'd been striving to find a way to "pursue" happiness that existed outside of her immediate world. The truth is that my dear friend had been in a conflicted marriage for the last twelve years of her life.

In her defense, she made several attempts to prevent discontent from extinguishing her dreams; one of which entailed using her childhood passion of becoming a celebrity photographer. But it was the burdensome distraction of despair that kept her from realizing her aspirations to their fullest potential. The harsh reality is that she'd spent much of those twelve years waiting for the right time to save money for a divorce; to buy or rent the right house she could afford yet would accommodate three growing boys. Her thinking was that when this happened, she'd then be able to invest the right amount of time and energy into her aspirations of becoming an entrepreneur. Another justification she maintained for living such an inert existence was the idea that people would think negatively of her if she were a divorced, single mother. Hence the reason she spent much of her time waiting for her husband to leave; waiting for her finances to get better; waiting for a miracle to take place so that she could have the life she truly desired. Thus, she'd ultimately be enabled to escape her miserable existence without being perceived an unfit mother to her children for breaking up the family. It is safe to conclude that she never quite understood how waiting merely sanctioned her need to carry out the façade and nothing more. In the end, the time she lost was a heavy price to pay for the sake of an image.

Finally, one year prior to her illness, my beloved friend managed to muster up the ambition to learn the business of photography. Wisely, she decided to use this knowledge to raise the money she needed to meet her goals and live the life she'd desired to live for quite some time. After forty-seven years, she was finally beginning to take the steps necessary to move – outward, onward and upward. I couldn't have been more proud or happier for her. Unfortunately, two days before she was to divorce herself from her husband, from the stress caused by a failing marriage, from tension and toxins that had been poisoning her home environment and from the grief that had held her hostage for far too long, my friend was diagnosed with a terminal illness.

I am sure you can fathom the anger she may have felt about being robbed of her chance to be happy. Because of her disappointment, she gave up on life at the moment of diagnosis. One would imagine that she would use the anger to as fuel to fight for life; to fight to live happily for the remainder of her days; to live and fulfill all of the dreams that had been nestled in her heart for the better part of her healthy years. As her biggest cheerleader, I tried my damndest to encourage my friend to go on trips, to go for walks and appreciate the life she had left. I tried my best to push her to do the little things that made life matter when she was healthy. Yet, bitterness caused her to shut down. I regretfully say that the only time she left the house was to receive her treatments and attend her weekly checkups. Seldom did she leave the confines of her house to engage in activities that would arouse joy and gratitude – no shopping, no photography adventures, no trips… NOTHING.

Until then, I'd never witnessed anything so sad, so disheartening.

Her reasoning: I have to get my rest. If I rest, then I could get healthy. Then I can have lunch with my friends, go to a beach, or go for a drive to the park with my boys. Again, she was waiting for the right time. She lived – or neglected to live – those nine months relying on whatever hope she could maintain, waiting to hear the doctor say, "You are healed, you can have your life back." That day never came. Needless to say, I can only imagine there to be more regret, anger and disappointment in her heart when the doctor informed her that she would not survive her battle.

Luckily, this angel had made an impact on so many people – friends and family – throughout her life. For we were the ones who visited her, brought her gifts, made her laugh and smile; we picked her up when she no longer had the strength to carry on. Now in the memory of her last smiles, her last laughs and even her last days, I still wish she'd chosen differently – to fight harder and to smile wider. It was MY desire, however. And I came to accept that this was her process and not my own. I had to finally accept that each person responds to life's trials differently. One of the hardest things I've ever had to do was remain conscious of my emotions throughout and after this ordeal. I fight hard not to grow angry as result of my own concept of survival. Tears fill my eyes as I struggle with trying to understand why she neglected to choose to do things that would make her last moments unforgettable. But no amount of begging could have changed her mind then, and it definitely could not change things when she eventually took her last breath. Yet still, through the sadness, I am at least inspired by the visions of the several hundred people who flocked to her funeral to celebrate her life.

People make choices. We don't always understand them. We don't always know what is going on the inside of them. We may not even know how we would act if we found ourselves in the same predicament. But what we can do, ladies, is try to make best of the life we DO have NOW, so that time is not lost.

It is because of this encounter with death – and life, depending on your perspective – that I feel compelled to move gently into this segment of my evolution of self. It was one thing to walk away from the experience fueled by all the gifts and clarifications that come with loss, all of which ultimately helped me to understand the concept and the power of now. Yet it would have been another thing to walk the face of this Earth hoarding all that I'd been enlightened enough to ascertain consequent to this account. How could I keep this to myself? What good would it do? After the funeral, after all the empathy and sympathy granted to me by friends and loved ones subsided, I was left alone to deal with my newly changed reality. There I stood, drowning in sorrow, standing on the edge of a cliff, on the brink of allowing pain to consume me. If I was going to turn this experience into something constructive, I was going to have to make some profound decisions in my life. If you have ever dealt with the loss of a loved one – and this was my first time – you can relate to the battle of fighting the urge to succumb to the sadness derived from the thought of moving on with life without your loved one. I had no idea how I was going to do it, especially with a big, gaping wound on my heart.

An interesting thing happened to me the day after my friend's memorial. I was listening to a speaker talk about the instances in her life that catapulted her into change, going from depressed drug addict to a renowned author. She shared with us listeners how the life-altering moment of enlightenment in her life came the day she lost her mother. It was then that I heard her say (paraphrasing): "We as humans have a tendency to feel pain and suffering when we see our loved ones go. We cry at their memories or whenever we feel their absence. Thus, we internalize what we are feeling in those instances and attribute it to pain; it is through this perception of pain that we suffer from loss. When my mother took her last breath, I chose not to suffer. To do this, I had to change my outlook. As I saw my mother lying there, staring into her eyes, silently realizing that her soul had made its departure, I could not stand to feel pain. Instead, I decided to perceive those moments of pain differently than I normally would have. I turned what felt like loss into feelings of love."

The author changed the paradigm about her experiences and instead of feeling excruciating grief, she taught herself to feel love and appreciation for having had the chance to share a portion of her life with her mother. Naturally, I was inspired to do the same thing. Once my grieving subsided, I decided to turn my

259

pain into love, and to use that love as the fuel I needed to become more productive in my life. I used the inspiration of my friend's life – including her success and her failures – to reach out to people around the world, so that they too could be enlightened and inspired to take control of their own lives.

Initially, I had mixed feelings about her departure. I was angry (I wished she'd fought a little harder to live; I had difficulty accepting that it was all a matter of opinion), confused, hurt, sad, happy (that she was no longer suffering), afraid (living life without my friend seemed so foreign) and at times, lost. However, as I began to contemplate the author's words, I found myself discovering a sense of joy. I began to accept that God knew what he was doing all along when He made our – my friend and me – paths cross. His purpose for my being a part of her life was so that I could contribute to the many smiles she had throughout it, especially in her last days. Her purpose was to share her experience (death) with me so that I would be empowered to be everything I dream to be and to try to avoid making the same mistakes she made. It was through this life changing experience that I am able to understand and grasp the concept that every one of us could be considered failures if we leave this life never having achieved and/or realized any of our dreams and goals. For that I am grateful. I may not achieve every one of my goals that I've set for myself going forward, "but" I am going to try my best.

"The pursuit of happiness" is a well-known cliché that is used quite often in parables or tales of inspiration. In fact, I used it once or twice in this book as a means of getting you to align yourself with the start of your journey towards success. The truth of the matter, my friend, is that there is no such thing as a pursuit of happiness. If I learned anything from my friend's passing, I learned that happiness is either in you or it isn't. So, here is another important lesson: your road to happiness should be a rather short one. All you have to do is look within. Inside of you is where you will find all you need to make self-actualization a possibility. Now, hopefully you can see why putting off something you desire – whether it is starting a family, taking a cooking class, or building a business from the ground up – is detrimental to the fruition of your entire existence. Turning within to "pursue your happiness" is worth every bit of effort it will take to help you realize your intended self.

About the Author

Kimberly E. Banks was born in raised in Los Angeles, California. She first began to show her creative talents in the discipline of art at the age of five, when she began drawing pictures with a box of assorted colored crayons. Since those early years, she has developed into a well-respected artist, known for her patented "bricking" style technique. It was through her desire to create astounding stories in her eye catching illustrations that enabled

Kimberly to develop a passion for writing. It became another means for painting more detailed images through word usage.

Because of the many adversities she has faced and overcome, both as a child and as an adult, Ms. Banks believes she has a special "calling" in life to minister to others with similar backgrounds through her literature.

Ms. Banks uses her pen to invite others into her world through her novels, short stories, and poetry. By blending fictional works with stories of her life experiences, she hopes to encourage others who may face comparable situations by demonstrating that when the will and spirit is strong, success is possible even when the odds seem insurmountable.

Ms. Banks mission is focused on creating a collection of works that centers on elevating the image of women and children, as well as, uplift the human spirit as a whole. Ms. Banks' sole desire is to write content that provoke readers to be accountable for their lives and arriving to their intended destinations; to search deep within their souls in order to find ways to contribute to healing society. Specifically through her children's books, Ms. Banks seeks to reach those who may be among the bullied, the teased, the insecure, the less fortunate, and the playground outcast. Thus, each project she writes enables survivors – adult or children, or the loved ones of survivors, to understand that they are not alone in this world; that maybe even the girl next door could be going through the same exact thing. Even more importantly, she encourages her readers to believe that they too can make it through to see a brighter day. Each project teaches life lessons such as compassion, perseverance, acceptance, humility, and sisterhood. It is her mission to reminder readers of their gifts, talent and passions so that they too can achieve each and every one of their heart's desires.

Upcoming Heartistic Motivation Titles

Upcoming Books

Ascensions: Whispers of my Soul by Kimberly Banks

Mask Man (a children's title) by Kimberly Banks

Pieces of My Dreams: Volume I by Kimberly Banks

Pieces of My Dreams: Volume II by Kimberly Banks

Tauray's Wings Part I By Evonne De Jarnette

~~~~~~

Audio Books/Compilations

Let Go of your But! Narrated by Kimberly Banks

Let Go of your But! Affirmation CD by Kimberly Banks

~~~~~~

More coming from the Let Go of Your But! Series

Let Go of Your But! Reaching your Full Potential

Let Go of Your But! Healing Relationshps

Let Go of Your But! Fitness and Health

Let Go of Your But! Manifesting your Professional Vision - Career & Business

We hope you enjoyed this inspirational book. If you'd like to learn more about the Let Go Of Your But! Movement, visit www.LetGoOfYourBut.com. For more about Heartistic Motivation visit www.HeartisticMotivation.com

Are excuses keeping you from living a vision, a dream, a passion, or a need for change

LET GO OF YOUR BUT!

w/Vision Coach & Author Kimberly E. Banks

265

Get Help

Mastering New Skillsets.

Getting Proactive. Breaking through Challenges!

Health & Well Being
Writing Coaching for Women
Vision/Dream Building Enrichment
Personal and Professional Enrichment

Call now and get your FREE sample session and a copy of

Let Go Of Your But! Little Book of Principles

Register for one-on-one sessions, group sessions, telephone coaching, programs and courses.

Books and apparel Available NOW on www.LetGoOfYourBut.com.

Kimberly E. Banks wants to partner with you!!
www.LetGoOfYourBut.com
management@heartisticmotivation.com   or   (678)999-6337

www.ingramcontent.com/pod-product-compliance
Lightning Source LLC
Chambersburg PA
CBHW030918090426
42737CB00007B/239